THE SECRET DIARY OF A COMPANY SECRETARY

THE UNTOLD TRUTHS OF FTSE BOARDROOMS
RETOLD BY ERIKA ELIASSON-NORRIS

CONTENTS

INTRODUCTION	01
WHY THIS BOOK EXISTS	03
WHAT YOU WILL LEARN	04
CHAPTER 1 – TRUTH, GRIT AND PURPOSE	09
CHAPTER 2 – MAYHEM IN A SUIT	25
CHAPTER 3 – CHAOS, CONTROL AND CREDIBILITY	43
CHAPTER 4 – BREAKING THE MOULD	67
CHAPTER 5 – A JOURNEY WITHOUT A MAP	87
CHAPTER 6 – DEADLINES AND DOLLAR SIGNS	105
CHAPTER 7 – THE NEVER-ENDING JUGGLE	129
CHAPTER 8 – DANCING WITH GIANTS	151
LETTER TO FUTURE LEADERS	174
APPENDIX	177
A BRIEF HISTORY OF THE ROLE OF THE COMPANY SECRETARY	177
BECOMING A COMPANY SECRETARY IN THE UK: A PATHWAY TO GOVERNANCE LEADERSHIP	182
ACKNOWLEDGEMENTS	186

INTRODUCTION

Thank you for buying this book, together we can change attitudes towards what should be a pivotal role in every organisation; the role of the Chartered Company Secretary or Chartered Governance Professional.

This book does not contain my story – that's one for another day. What follows reflects the stories of eight Group Company Secretaries, my peers, whose experiences and perspectives capture the evolving nature of our profession. As someone who secured the top governance job as a FTSE 250 Group Company Secretary at the age of 32 – the youngest in my field at the time – and who has since been recognised as Governance Professional of the Year (2022) and appointed as the Governance Assessor to the Post Office Horizon IT Inquiry, I bring a deep understanding of the role. But here, I am simply the observer and narrator of stories that deserve to be heard.

When a job can affect the lives of millions of people and yet few understand its true significance, someone needs to speak up and bring the Company Secretary or Governance Professional role to life. William Shakespeare wrote in Romeo and Juliet, 'What's in a name?' and I too believe that regardless of how misleading a job title is, it's true value exists independently of those words. There is so much more to it – and these stories must be told.

It all started with my first job, fresh out of university, as a Trainee Company Secretary. A job title that misled everyone into either instantly switching off – the 'boredom factor' – or believing it was purely administrative (even at networking events with board directors and executive colleagues who work alongside a Company Secretary). No one knew the importance of the role, what the holder of the position does and what can go wrong if it is not done well. Interestingly, according to a survey by the Chartered Governance Institute UK & Ireland, 58% of board members believe the Company Secretary is undervalued by senior leadership[1].

Still, in the wake of the UK Post Office Horizon IT Inquiry and countless other newsworthy organisational scandals, few understand that governance failures are the root cause. I would even go so far as to say that this book might open a few Company Secretaries' eyes to what the work might involve and address the age-old challenge of the role being undervalued by our peers.

The effect of action or inaction around governance can be the downfall of an organisation and bring about the destruction of an otherwise well-managed career as a director. Having seen firsthand the devastation of getting it wrong, I owe it to my profession to take proactive steps to address this and raise the profile of the role, something I will continue to do for many years to come.

This is not a vanity project. I don't need to make myself or the contributors to this book feel that what we do is worthwhile – We know it is. Instead, I want to raise awareness of the unsung heroes whose stories are told through the stories in this book and others whose stories have not yet been heard, who carry out the governance role under the title of Company Secretary.

As you read these stories, I invite you to reflect on the people behind the profession. The stories in this book are drawn from interviews with real people. Each chapter introduces a different individual with their own story to tell, personal experiences shaped by the realities of a complex and often misunderstood role. While they have chosen to remain anonymous, their reflections are honest, moving and at times unexpected. I am grateful to each of them for sharing their moments of laughter, challenge and insight with me.

It is your time to be heard. May your stories inform, entertain and encourage others to look at governance with fresh eyes, and force directors and our peers to reflect on how they value the role of the Company Secretary.

Why This Book Exists

The profession of the Company Secretary – or Governance Professional, as it's increasingly known – is both ancient and evolving. It operates behind the scenes, by design. We are the keepers of the boardroom's confidences, the quiet conscience of corporate leadership, and the unseen thread stitching together integrity, process, and purpose. But therein lies the paradox: our greatest strength – discretion – has often become our greatest obstacle to recognition.

In early 2024, in a quiet corner of a bustling meeting room in Marylebone London, a group of exceptional Company Secretaries and Governance Professionals gathered under the banner of a Beyond Governance roundtable. We came together not just as colleagues, but as guardians of one of the most misunderstood and underappreciated professions in the corporate world. What began as a routine discussion about the future of our profession quickly turned into something far more personal – and urgent.

One question kept echoing through the room: *Why does no one know what we do?* It was a familiar frustration. Many of us had experienced it first-hand: standing at social events, drink in hand, trying to explain our roles to friends, family or strangers, only to be met with puzzled expressions, polite nods, or outright confusion. "So... you take minutes?" they might ask, as if that captured the essence of a job that can involve advising boards, navigating crises, and quietly influencing the strategic direction of some of the biggest companies in the world.

I made a promise in that room. I vowed to change that.
This book is the beginning of that change. Not by shouting from the rooftops or crafting a PR campaign, but by lifting the metaphorical curtain and letting others see what we see. It is a collection of real stories, told by real professionals – anonymously, of course, because secrecy is not just part of the job, it is the whole job. These are the whispered truths of the boardroom: the egos, the ethical dilemmas, the moments of quiet influence, and the sheer, surprising variety of the tasks we undertake – often the jobs with no obvious home, and sometimes even those that should have one.

This is not an exposé. There are no scandalous revelations here. Instead, think of it as a lantern held up to the dark corners of a misunderstood world. These stories illuminate the vital, complex, and often deeply human work of governance. They reveal what it's like to walk among corporate giants and quietly shape the decisions that affect real everyday people — not from the spotlight, but from the shadows.

The 'Leadership Lessons' shared in this diary reflect my own experiences, insights, and evolving perspective in governance. They are personal observations drawn from my experiences of the boardroom and beyond.

To all who contributed their experiences: thank you for trusting me with your stories. Your voices, though unnamed, ring out with purpose here. And to the readers — those curious, perhaps sceptical, perhaps newly inspired — welcome. This is the world of governance as it truly is: unseen but essential, silent but powerful, humble but transformational.

This book is a call to awareness, a celebration of a profession, and — most of all — a step towards making sure that, next time someone asks *"What is it you do?"*, we'll have a very different conversation.

What You Will Learn

The Secret Diary of a Company Secretary offers a rare, candid window into one of the most misunderstood — and yet essential — roles in modern business. Whether you're a seasoned director, an emerging governance professional, or a student exploring your career path, this book will challenge your assumptions and deepen your understanding of life behind the boardroom door.

Inside these pages, you will discover:

1. What Governance Professionals Really Do
Go beyond the stereotypes of minute-taking and box-ticking to understand the true scope and depth of the governance role. Learn how company secretaries are critical to ensuring accountability, maintaining corporate integrity, and protecting organisational reputation.

2. The Hidden World of the Boardroom
Peek into the real dynamics that play out among elite directors, towering egos, and high-stakes decision-making. See how governance professionals navigate these spaces with diplomacy, discretion, and strength.

3. How Influence is Wielded Quietly but Powerfully
Uncover how governance professionals shape outcomes – not through formal authority, but through insight, timing, and trusted relationships. Learn what it means to be a strategic adviser in the room, not just a silent note-taker.

4. Candid Reflections from the Front Line
Through anonymised diary entries and stories, one chapter per individual, hear the lived experience of governance professionals who have seen it all – from ethical dilemmas to organisational dysfunction, and moments of deep professional pride.

5. Why Governance Matters More Than Ever
In an age of corporate scrutiny, ESG expectations, and stakeholder activism, understand why the role of the company secretary is evolving from compliance custodian to culture shaper and leadership enabler.

6. How to Step into the Role with Confidence
Whether you're aspiring to the profession or already working within it, this book will equip you with the mindset, resilience, and clarity to make a real impact and thrive in a role that demands both courage and care.

This book won't just tell you what a company secretary is. It will show you – through stories, moments, and the unfiltered reality of a profession that deserves to be seen. So come with me on a journey – into the boardroom, behind closed doors, and into the heart of a role built on trust, discretion, and quiet influence. Whether you're encountering this world for the first time or seeing it through fresh eyes, you're about to discover the powerful, often hidden story of governance.

CHAPTER 1

CHAPTER 1

TRUTH, GRIT AND PURPOSE

Here I am, standing in the midst of a business that's in its early stages of maturity, not every governance control is in place – and frankly, not every one of them is needed. It's like being on a rickety train that's upgrading each aspect of itself as it moves along the track; not the smoothest ride, but there's progress.

I've worked in far more mature operations, but I've come to love the challenge of adapting like a chameleon to whatever environment I'm thrown into. The people are good, the potential is there, and I find a certain thrill in shaping something from the ground up.

It's funny when I think back to those early days, when you're at A-levels, sitting in front of a career adviser who clearly has no clue what to do with you. I remember ticking boxes on some careers test that was supposed to map out my future, and it kept spitting out the same answer: business, business administration. I wasn't sold. Then, I chose law for my degree. Not because I had any aspirations of becoming a lawyer – not in a million years. I just figured it was slightly more respectable than some other career choices available at the time.

Law was interesting, sure. It was challenging, hard work, and I liked the intellectual grind of it. The tutors were good, the people were decent. But the funny thing was, while I was doing my degree, I met this guy – a mature student like me – who had no intention of becoming a lawyer either. His ambition was something I had barely heard of at the time: he wanted to be a company secretary.

He explained his reasoning, and while it didn't spark anything for me at the time, it planted a seed. It's pretty common for company secretaries to have a law degree, and some have pursued a career in law first. The legal and ethical aspects of the role benefit hugely from having someone in the role who has good legal knowledge.

After university, I took a job as a legal assistant at a renewable energy company. The lawyer I worked for was also the company secretary, and soon enough, I was exposed to both worlds. One day, she came to me with a choice: did I want to pursue law, or did I want to dive into the company secretarial side?

The decision was instant. "I don't want to be a lawyer," I said, without hesitation. And the CEO – who had clearly been watching me – said, "You light up when you do the governance work. You hate drafting contracts, but you thrive when you're in the boardroom, organising, directing, making things happen." He was right. The law bored me, but the company secretarial work? That was exhilarating.

Eventually, that CEO sold his company, and I found myself out of a job, I needed to carve out a new path. That's when I came across an article about alternative careers for lawyers, and right there at the top of the list was company secretary. It felt like the universe had aligned again. I contacted a recruiter on the Monday, had an interview by Wednesday, and on Friday I was signed up to start my exams and my first proper plc company secretary role at a real estate company. And just like that, the pieces fell into place.

Looking back, it's clear to me that I was destined for this. Being a company secretary just made sense in a way that law never did. Those first five years were transformative – I learned the ropes, passed my postgraduate exams and threw myself into every aspect of the role.

It wasn't just a job; it became my passion. The challenges, the organisation, the responsibility of keeping everything on track – I thrived on it. And from that point on, there was no looking back. This was what I was meant to do.

Keep your eye on the target

I'm very driven – give me a list of goals, deadlines, AGMs, and reports to hit, and I'm in my element. I thrive on the constant cycle of tasks in the company secretarial world, plus the unexpected curveballs that always seem to pop up. It's never boring. For me, what drew me to this role were the parts of law that really challenge your mind – things like the Companies Act. That's where I found real satisfaction.

I'm outspoken, and I'd like to think I have a strong moral compass. Being a company secretary gives me the chance to tap into that, whether it's ensuring fairness and inclusion or making sure things are done equitably. It's a role that allows collaboration, unlike the more cutthroat nature of law. I'm not built for competitive environments – I'm happy to let my boss shine, she's brilliant and deserves it.

I love to share knowledge, learn from others, and work together. I know that the kind of competition you find in other professions would have chewed me up and spat me out, so I found my place in this world of governance, where collaboration trumps competition.

LEADERSHIP LESSON

What sets the governance profession apart is the lack of ego. At the top of the field are clever, principled individuals who are comfortable operating in ambiguity – They excel in the spaces where rules alone don't provide the answers – where judgement, nuance, and ethical clarity matter more than strict legal interpretation – and that's where governance professionals come into their own. They are guided not by self-interest, but by a strong ethical compass and a deep sense of responsibility to the organisations and communities they serve.

And then there's the exhibitionists

One of the more memorable (and cringeworthy) moments of my career as a company secretary, involved an AGM where a certain shareholder had, let's just say, a tendency to get a little too comfortable. I had received a letter beforehand from his medical team, explaining his condition – diagnosed as *exhibitionism*. Apparently, he had an uncontrollable urge to disrobe in public settings, and the AGM was no exception.

The real challenge was preparing for it, knowing this could happen, and making sure we had protocols in place to handle it discreetly. We were trying to maintain the dignity of the meeting while also being prepared for the unexpected.

When it inevitably happened, there was a moment of shock, but the team was ready. It was one of those situations where, afterward, you just had to laugh about it, because really, what else can you do? It's certainly not the usual company secretary task you'd expect, but it's a reminder that this job throws some truly unpredictable curveballs!

Adviser not colleague

I've found that working closely with boards feels less like being part of a team and more like being a trusted confidant. Whether it's the Chair, the Audit Committee Chair, or the Remuneration Chair, those relationships are built on straight, honest conversations, often behind the scenes. It's not about the usual team dynamic – it's more about influence and being someone, they can confide in.

I was brought in specifically for my listed company expertise. Supporting the Chair to get things up to standard isn't always glamorous, but it's where you have those crucial, confidential talks about how to elevate governance.

It's not just about aiming to be a top-tier company – it's about knowing what good governance looks like because you've been trained by the best. And just as important is recognising what doesn't look good. That's all part of the learning curve as a company secretary, and those lessons are just as valuable as the wins.

I've been incredibly lucky in my career to work with boards that have a strong moral compass and genuinely want to do the right thing. That's probably why I've enjoyed being a company secretary so much – it's not just about the mechanics of governance; it's about the strength it takes to be the lone voice in the room when it's needed. And trust me, that happens more often than you'd think.

I've had to stand up to bosses, to be that voice of reason or caution, and I'd like to believe that in the right environment, the right board, you should never be afraid to speak up. If you are, you're probably not going to make it as a company secretary.

Throughout my career, I've been in rooms where, even in the most difficult situations, the board was committed to doing the right thing. But let me tell you, it's not always smooth sailing. I once found myself in the middle of a storm – a board blindsided by a Financial Conduct Authority (FCA) Arrow visit.

For those unfamiliar, this is when the UK's financial regulator descends on your company like a hawk, tearing through every corner to see if you're playing by the rules. They scrutinise everything – are you managing risks? Are you treating customers fairly? Is your business a ticking timebomb for the financial system? It's as intense as it sounds, and this particular visit. It was brutal.

There were 875,000 reported cases of work-related stress, depression, or anxiety in 2022/23.[2]

We weren't talking about a slap on the wrist. The FCA unearthed all sorts of issues – misconduct that wasn't even on the board's radar. And here's the kicker: they weren't corrupt, they weren't trying to game the system.

They genuinely thought what they were doing was just business as usual. But ignorance doesn't get you off the hook. The stakes were enormously high, and my job was to guide them through this minefield, knowing that every step could trigger another explosion.

This wasn't just about compliance breaches; it was about real lives hanging in the balance. People were breaking under the pressure. One of the most harrowing moments was when someone – someone we all knew – took their own life during this investigation.

That's when it hit me like a freight train: being a company secretary isn't just about governance, it's about holding the line when everything's falling apart. We're not just pushing papers; we're dealing with the raw, gritty human cost that no one talks about. And in those moments, you realise just how much hangs in the balance every time you step into that boardroom.

The tragic crashes of Boeing's 737 MAX aircraft in 2018 and 2019 claimed the lives of 346 people and was linked to significant governance failures within the company and regulatory bodies.[3]

LEADERSHIP LESSON

Every boardroom decision carries human consequences, often unseen but deeply felt. Governance leaders must balance precision with empathy – because behind every policy, process, or paper trail is a person, a livelihood, a real-world outcome that demands care as much as compliance.

Predatory behaviour

The worst situation I've ever been through – and perhaps the reason I'm so fiercely protective of women in the workplace – was when I had a boss, early in my career, who was a predator.

I was young and naive, just starting out, and when I turned down his advances, my life became a living hell for years. He made it his mission to undermine me at every turn, to crush my spirit. But I wouldn't let him. I dug deep, endured the torment, and came out stronger on the other side. That experience lit a fire in me.

It's why I'm so passionate about lifting women up and supporting them – because I've been there. And what I love about this younger generation of women in the workplace is that they won't stand for it. If someone tried that now, they'd whistle-blow so fast it would make your head spin. And I love that.

Studies show that 52% of women in the UK have experienced sexual harassment at work, encompassing behaviours such as unwelcome jokes, comments about appearance, unwanted touching, and sexual advances.[4]

The company secretary is also typically the person writing the whistleblowing policy and anti-bullying and harassment policy which is empowering in itself. I love that we've come so far that women are finding their voices and speaking up, demanding the respect they deserve.

Fifteen years ago, it wasn't like that. Back then, you swallowed your pride, kept your head down, and hoped to survive. But times have changed and thank goodness.

When I look at the news, I know that this sort of thing does still happen. But the tide is turning, and I'm committed to making sure that every woman feels safe in the workplace, safe in society, and supported no matter what.

It all comes back to that moral compass – standing up for what's right, even when it's hard. That's the kind of strength I want to see in every boardroom.

Lifting people up

One of the most valuable lessons I've learned – and one I pass on to every junior starting out – is this: don't take things personally. It's easier said than done, I know, but the sooner you master that, the more you'll enjoy both your career and your life.

As a company secretary, we deal with senior executives and board directors all the time, it could even be on your first day as a trainee, and not everything will go your way. People will challenge you, sometimes unfairly. But it's not about you, it's about the job, and the more you can separate the two, the stronger you'll be.

Bringing your authentic self to work is another key part of thriving in this field. It says a lot about the culture of a company when you can do that. Yes, it takes bravery to be yourself, especially when you're dealing with boards made up of people from different generations or backgrounds.

Sometimes, their views can feel outdated, even uncomfortable. But part of your job is to educate and guide them – sometimes it's as simple as pulling someone aside after a meeting and gently correcting them. Like one of our NEDs who, in the most graceful way, reminded a board member that we don't say "ethnic minority," we say "global majority." It was a small but powerful moment of learning.

Being a company secretary isn't just about rules and regulations; it's about standing up when something's wrong. I wasn't always vocal when I was younger, and I regret not speaking up when I had the chance.

You don't always have to call things out in front of everyone – sometimes it's a quiet word with the Chair or Audit Committee Chair. And that's why your moral compass is so important in this role.

LEADERSHIP LESSON:
Success in governance isn't just about knowledge – it's about composure, authenticity, and moral clarity. The strongest leaders know when to speak up, when to step in quietly, and how to lead with integrity in every room they enter.

Amidst the pandemic times

When the pandemic hit, it was like a bomb going off inside every boardroom and executive suite across the country. Crisis management became the name of the game, and suddenly, who sat on the 'gold committee' – the team responsible for navigating the business through uncharted waters – became a matter of survival.

As a company secretary, you weren't just sitting on the sidelines. You were in the room, right there in the thick of it. You were the one ensuring the ship stayed on course amidst the chaos.

The pandemic was a wake-up call for so many, and I'd bet that most company secretaries found themselves involved in some capacity on their company's crisis-management team. We might not be the ones pulling the trigger on the big decisions, but we're the ones gathering the evidence, providing support, and laying the groundwork for those decisions to be made.

Whether it was organising the facts, collaborating across teams, or ensuring that the process stayed on track, our role was pivotal. We were the steady hands behind the scenes, making sure everything that needed to happen could happen, even if it meant making the hardest choices of all.

The myth of two-for-one: Why lawyers can't be company secretaries

Let's face it, the role of a company secretary requires complete impartiality – something that lawyers, by the very nature of their job, often struggle to maintain. As a company secretary, you're there to serve the best interests of the company as a whole, not to focus on the technicalities or the personal stakes of any one individual.

Your job is to be the voice of reason, to ensure that what's being done is right for the greater good of the organisation, not just to help executives exercise their stock options at the optimal moment. This neutrality is crucial, and it's something lawyers can find difficult, especially when they themselves may be PDMRs (Persons Discharging Managerial Responsibilities) with their own financial interests tied into the company's success.

Lawyers, by training, are more focused on the technical and legal details. Their role is to protect the company from legal risk, which is absolutely vital, particularly during crises. But a company secretary approaches things differently – logically, practically, with a broader view of governance that transcends legal technicalities. The interpretation of governance issues requires not just legal expertise but a deep understanding of the company's overall strategy and ethical standing. That's a very different skill set.

I've seen environments where the general counsel and the company secretary respect and complement each other perfectly – each sticking to their respective roles, ensuring that legal and governance functions operate smoothly side by side. Sadly, though, that's rare.

The reality is, truly exceptional lawyers don't aspire to be company secretaries. They are laser-focused on their legal careers, climbing to partner level, mastering their field. On the flip side, there are some lawyers who may not find success reaching the top levels of their profession and view the joint role of general counsel and company secretary as a fallback, a 'Plan B'. For companies, it might seem like a bargain – two roles for the price of one – but that's a false economy.

A lawyer who's already swamped with legal work simply doesn't have the time, or the breadth of perspective, to fulfil the responsibilities of a company secretary effectively. During times like recessions, when resources are tight, a split role with two individuals only becomes more challenging for executive to buy into.

The truth is these roles are distinct for a reason. A company secretary isn't just a legal function – it's a governance one, grounded in impartiality, collaboration, and the ability to see the bigger picture. No matter how good a lawyer is, that independent perspective is something they often can't and shouldn't be expected to bring to the table.

LEADERSHIP LESSON

Governance leadership demands impartiality and a panoramic view of the organisation's best interests. It's not a fallback role; it's a distinct and vital function that keeps the board grounded in integrity and aligned with its strategy and purpose.

No room at the top?

It's a bittersweet reality in our field that the top governance roles are often out of reach for those of us who aren't lawyers. The positions are frequently combined with general counsel roles, and if, like me, you haven't done your Legal Practice Course, the ceiling feels very real.

I've been a deputy for over ten years, across three different companies, and while I love being a company secretary, I can't stay at this level forever. It's not that I'm not capable – I know my job inside and out – but after a decade in the same role, the challenge just isn't there anymore.

I've seen incredibly talented people, bright minds with so much potential, hit the same wall simply because they don't have that legal qualification. It's frustrating because their ability to excel as a company secretary isn't in question, yet the path upwards seems blocked. It's not a complaint, just an observation about the reality of our industry.

There comes a point where you start to wonder, what's next? If the only way forward is through a door that's closed to you, maybe it's time to find a different door altogether. It's a tough decision, especially when you're passionate about what you do, but we all need to feel like there's room to grow and be challenged.

Joy is seeing others thrive

Let me tell you a little secret about being a company secretary. It's not just about governance and regulations – though that's certainly a part of it – but it's about being at the heart of so many different things.

I've found myself in roles where, on any given day, I'm bouncing from investor relations meetings to sitting on a panel with the CFO, helping pick the right broker for the company. And trust me, it's not as simple as just finding the best numbers guy – it's about saying, "Hey, we need more diversity here. We can't have a panel full of old white men." And being that voice in the room that advocates for real inclusion? It's empowering.

That's the magic of this career – it's a long-lasting one because, wherever you go, you tend to find yourself amongst people who are fair, supportive, and just plain nice. And I don't mind if someone else gets the job I was eyeing, because if they're the right person for it, good for them.

Watching people grow, supporting their success – that's what I love most. Sure, I enjoy the business conversations with my chair, the high-level strategic talks, but the real joy comes from seeing others thrive. That's what makes this role so special.

LEADERSHIP LESSON

True leadership isn't measured by how far you climb, but by how many people rise with you. There's strength in creating space for others to grow – and real fulfilment comes from knowing you've helped unlock their potential.

A seat at our table for all

One of the things I absolutely love about being a company secretary is that you get to deal with *everyone* – from the top brass to the person sorting the post. And, you know what? We treat everyone the same. Whether it's the girl at reception who's helped me sort out a board meeting or the guy in the post room. A quick "thank you, you're amazing" can make their day, and that's what I love.

One of the most rewarding aspects of being a company secretary is overseeing share schemes, especially those for all employees. It's not just about compliance or paperwork – it's about witnessing the tangible impact on people's lives.

When their investment pays off, it can mean buying a first car or taking that long-dreamed holiday. Being part of that journey and seeing how a company's share scheme translates into real rewards is incredibly fulfilling.

The best moments are when employees you've never met thank you, saying things like, "I used my share scheme money to buy a new kitchen," or "We're finally going on our dream holiday." These stories are a powerful reminder that the work we do reaches far beyond the boardroom – it's about creating opportunities that change lives. That's what makes me passionate about this role.

Then there are the other sides of the job, like helping to choose the charity partner or recommending a new direction for the company's ESG (Environment, Social and Governance) policies. Those are the moments when you feel like you're contributing something more significant – not just ticking boxes but finding the right fit and watching it flourish.

Between 2019 and 2022 companies with robust ESG initiatives have experienced a 9.1% increase in profitability.[5]

Every day is a bit of an adventure – whether it's teaching people how to prepare board papers or guiding them through the ins and outs of governance. It's all about helping. That's where we differ from lawyers, I think. There's a real passion for supporting people in this role, for being there when they need you.

And, oh, the laughter, I laugh every day! In my company we've got an all-female leadership team and it's so much fun. We don't always laugh because things are going well, but hey, when you're dealing with the things we do, sometimes all you can do is laugh. In this job I think you need a bit of a dry, quirky sense of humour; that's what gets us through the madness. This job can be absolutely nuts at times, but we do it together – and we laugh a lot along the way.

LEADERSHIP LESSON

One of the most powerful traits in governance is the ability to talk to everyone – and truly listen. Whether it's the Chair or the receptionist, mutual respect matters. You'll call on people across every level of the business, often when it matters most. Treating everyone with dignity isn't just the right thing to do – it builds the relationships that make everything else possible.

Be careful who you step on to reach the top

There's one story that will always stick with me, and it perfectly sums up why resilience and kindness matter in this field. One of my past bosses… let's just say he wasn't exactly a beacon of decency.

He had this habit of being particularly unkind to one of the juniors who he thought was insignificant. But time has a funny way of flipping the script. That same person rose through the ranks, eventually becoming the CEO! And wouldn't you know it – the first thing he did was serve my old boss a hefty slice of karma. It's a perfect reminder that every dog has its day, and if you lead with cruelty, it'll come back to bite you in ways you can't predict.

That's what's fascinating about being a company secretary. If you stick around long enough, you see the full cycle of board members – people come and go, evolve, and sometimes even circle back in unexpected ways. It's like watching a play unfold from the wings, witnessing the ups and downs of leadership from a vantage point that few get to experience.

But it's not just about the cycle – it's about finding your strength and resilience in this often-daunting environment. One company I worked in was heavily male dominated, it had a macho atmosphere, and the women had to stand their ground, be strong, and rely on one another to get through it.

In those moments, you find an ally – someone in that boardroom who has your back – and that's when your resilience really shines. It's not just about surviving; it's about quietly influencing, knowing you're not alone, and standing firm with confidence even when the odds feel stacked against you.

Women occupy 40.2% of board positions in the FTSE350 and 33.5% of leadership roles.[6]

Sure, the boardroom can be intimidating. Some of the directors are older, well-educated, and have spent decades crafting their careers. At times, it feels like they're speaking a different language, so polished and self-assured. But when you find that one friend in the room, someone who supports your voice, it makes all the difference. That's where your power comes from – not just in what you say, but in knowing you have the strength, the resilience, and the support to keep pushing forward.

LEADERSHIP LESSON

The boardroom may be daunting, but your greatest power often lies in the allies you find, the kindness you show, and the steady presence you hold as the cycles of leadership unfold.

Do you have to be posh?

I used to feel out of place in the boardroom, surrounded by these incredibly posh, well-educated people who were much older and loved to pick apart my grammar because it wasn't how they would write it. But then I realised something a brilliant mentor once told me: *You are the diversity in that room.* They need you far more than you need them, because without you, they all look the same, talk the same, and think the same.

LEADERSHIP LESSON

To avoid the trap of groupthink, some leaders follow the Tenth Man Rule: when nine agree, one must challenge. Even if they personally support the decision, their role is to probe, question, and uncover blind spots – because strong governance isn't about consensus alone, it's about the courage to test it.[7]

I've found myself in more than a few rich boys' clubs over the years, and it's obvious when my voice doesn't fit in. I'm vocal, I'll speak my mind, and you can see the discomfort it causes. It's not subtle – you're made to feel like an outsider. Sure, everyone tries to get along with HR, investor relations, and finance because that's part of the job, but there's a definite exclusivity that's hard to ignore.

What's frustrating is that this mentality isn't coming from the top. The leadership, in my experience, has never been like that – they're open and fair. But there's this layer just beneath, a sort of ingrained boys' club culture that hasn't been addressed. You see it when you're presenting or sharing ideas – there's eye-rolling, sniggering, little jabs that make it clear you're not part of the inner circle.

I've got a young woman on my team with a strong northern accent, and the way she's spoken to in boardrooms is shocking, despite her being incredibly bright and talented. This exclusionary behaviour comes from my generation and above – I don't see it in the younger crowd. There's hope for change as the younger generation moves up in the boardroom. The subtle exclusion that 'boys' from private schools use – it's there, and it's noted, and I have no problem calling it out. It's not just unhelpful, it's downright counterproductive.

Leading with intention

Wherever you are in your career, one thing remains true: it's crucial to make the next person's journey a little easier than your own. We've all faced challenges – some more subtle, some blatant – but the real mark of progress is how we lift others up along the way. Whether it's by calling out exclusionary behaviour, supporting younger colleagues, or simply sharing knowledge, we have the power to shape a better, fairer future. Every step we take to smooth the path for the next person helps create a workplace where talent, not background, drives success. Ultimately, that's how real change happens – one act of support at a time.

And here I am, having faced down those toughest challenges with grace, and come out on the other side stronger. Every win, every hard-fought victory, is a testament to that resilience. So, yes, I've seen the cycle, I've faced the intimidation, but I've also found my place – and I'm still standing.

CHAPTER 2

CHAPTER 2

MAYHEM IN A SUIT

If you'd asked me at seven what I wanted to be, I would have confidently said the captain of a ferry. Growing up by the sea, I was captivated by the daily comings and goings of the ferries. However, that dream was fleeting, quickly replaced by a passion for law and finance.

Upon graduating, the legal job market was fiercely competitive. It seemed everyone wanted to be a lawyer; there were hundreds of applicants for only a handful of trainee roles, as such jobs were limited unless you knew the 'right' people, and I didn't. Lacking the right connections, I faced the dilemma of self-funding my bar exams, a risk I couldn't afford.

A fortuitous interview with a top law firm, thanks to a friend's help, exposed me to the all-consuming life of a commercial lawyer. The sight of a sleeping bag under a desk made me realise this path wasn't for me – camping overnight in an office wasn't my idea of success (albeit there have been moments in my career when this seemed very likely… but it is never the 'norm').

From the post room to the boardroom

I truly believe that you never know the domino effect a decision can have on the rest of your life. I took a 'throwaway' student holiday job in the post room of a major retailer, and ended up staying there after graduation; a number of years later I met the company secretary and the secretarial team.

In this encounter I discovered my ideal role. It blended business law with governance and had varied responsibilities. As the most junior member of the team, I was enthused to have responsibility for the Chair's, CEO's and CFO's pay, tax and pensions and to draft key parts of external company reports on behalf of these same people. My written work was the voice of the company, and was read and reviewed by investors, shareholders and employees alike.

Legal issues, financial queries, operational snafus – you name it, the company secretarial team handles it, all while delivering a top-notch 'white glove' service. We might not always have the answers, but we sure know who to ask. The best teams make it look effortless, but when you're under-resourced, it's like trying to juggle flaming torches while riding a unicycle.

Being a company secretary is like riding a rollercoaster blindfolded – filled with challenges, triumphs, and moments that make you wonder if you've stumbled into a sitcom. From day one, I found myself knee-deep in the intricacies of the boardroom, gaining insights into the mysterious ways of executives. It's been an eye-opening journey through both business brilliance and blunders, offering a front-row seat to some of the most visionary leaders, alongside others who were, at times, utterly uninspiring.

I quickly learned that our governance function needed to be the ultimate 'one-stop shop' for directors – a bit like the concierge at a swanky hotel, but with more spreadsheets and fewer suitcases. It also became apparent very quickly that there was a chasm between the board of directors' understanding of my role and the reality of it; sometimes I was pulled far beyond the boundaries of my usual role, while at other times I was left out of key – often high-stakes – conversations on matters that sat firmly within the remit of governance.

LEADERSHIP LESSON
Governance leadership demands range, not routine. It's a role that spans legal, financial, operational, and relational spheres – requiring the agility to pivot, the insight to advise, and the steadiness to lead, often all in a single day.

A jack of all trades... and Master of Governance

Governance isn't confined to board packs and committee meetings. In practice, it's a full-contact sport – played out in unexpected places, from deserted car parks to PR disasters in the making. When things go off-script, Company Secretaries are often the ones quietly holding the line. These stories might raise a smile, but they also reveal the invisible threads that hold an organisation together. Because behind every calm exterior is someone juggling chaos, calling the right people, asking the right questions, and keeping everything from unravelling. That's what it really means to be a Master of Governance.

We once had to manage a situation where Irish Travelers set up camp in our store car park. It was a sensitive operation that involved issuing legal notices, coordinating with social services, and at times, involving the police. The process dragged on for six weeks, during which, store revenue plummeted as customers stayed away.

High stakes? Absolutely. It felt like a game of chess – only the pieces pitched tents and refused to budge. Governance is rarely a straight line. It shifts and evolves, and success often comes down to navigating complexity with skill, emotional intelligence, and a steady hand.

A 10% increase in a manager's emotional intelligence score was associated with a 7% improvement in overall business performance, including profitability.[8]

Then there were the abandoned cars. Some people think it's perfectly fine to leave their old clunkers in our car parks to avoid towing fees. One store skipped our usual protocol – like placing notices and checking with the DVLA – and had a car taken straight to the scrapyard. The plot twist?

The car's owner had been in the hospital after a heart attack in our store three weeks prior and came back to find her vehicle missing. I had to step in, apologise profusely, and manage the fallout, proving once again why our processes have to be meticulous; we can't have cars being crushed for no reason!

Another unforgettable incident took place during the planned grand opening of a new store on what had once been an old industrial site. The centrepiece of the launch was to be the demolition of a towering 250ft, 2,500-ton cooling tower – an iconic structure from the site's industrial past. A famous English steeplejack and television personality had been brought in to press the ceremonial button that would trigger the controlled demolition, turning the event into a symbolic moment of transformation. Everything had been meticulously planned: the cameras were set, the explosives primed, and the crowd expected the following day.

As part of final preparations, a routine test blast was carried out to confirm all systems were functioning correctly. But the tower had its own schedule. Without warning, it collapsed in its entirety, a full day ahead of plan. The immediate response was one of controlled urgency – teams quickly moved to verify that all staff and contractors were safely outside the exclusion zone, and thankfully, everyone was. The safety protocols worked exactly as they were meant to. Still, the surprise brought chaos in its own right: the demolition was over before the cameras had rolled, the event headliner was left without a stage, and our PR opportunity had quite literally crumbled. The steeplejack later described it in an interview as one of the most unexpected and dangerous situations he had encountered, though no injuries occurred.

What was supposed to be a PR win quickly spiralled into a full-blown farce, complete with a generous helping of explosives and a cooling tower that had a mind of its own. It's one of those moments where you laugh after the fact – but at the time, it was the stuff of nightmares. The lesson? Even the most carefully orchestrated plans can surprise you – and in governance, your crisis response is just as important as your preparation.

31% of businesses that have experienced a crisis reported that they would have communicated more effectively with stakeholders if given a second chance.[9]

Then there was the curious case of the children's ride-on cars – the kind you often see outside supermarkets and shopping centres. At first, no one thought much of them. But it turned out that someone had been placing these machines outside our stores, quietly tapping into our electricity supply and pocketing the profits. No contract, no permission, and no trace of who was behind it. It was a rogue setup hiding in plain sight.

The scheme only came to light when one of the machines was stolen. The store was suddenly invoiced by the very people running the unauthorised operation – prompting a cascade of questions and a scramble to make sense of what was going on. Untangling the mess felt like corporate detective work, equal parts baffling and bizarre.

Ah, and the joys of health and safety mishaps! One particular incident stands out as a prime example of the sheer absurdity we sometimes face. Picture this: a store decided to host a competition where customers could win a car. Sounds simple enough, right? Well, for some inexplicable reason, they thought it would be a brilliant idea to bring the car into the store during opening hours, instead of doing it when the store was closed.

So, imagine trying to manoeuvre this shiny prize car through the back door – because, of course, it wouldn't fit through the front. The sight of a car driving around the aisles of a store was already surreal, but it got even better. As they rounded a corner, they clipped the end stop – the display area where you stack all those tempting two-for-one cornflakes boxes. The car's bumper sent the entire display crashing down like a cereal avalanche, burying an unsuspecting shopper in a mountain of tumbling boxes.

And who, of all people, was this unfortunate soul under the mountain of cornflakes? None other than the health and safety officer of the local council!

There was absolutely nowhere to hide. The irony was almost too perfect, like something straight out of a comedy sketch. We had to stand there, trying to keep a straight face while the officer emerged from the debris, like a cornflake-covered statue of doom. Needless to say, the paperwork that followed was bureaucracy at its worst.

A common misconception links corporate governance with unnecessary bureaucracy, but these two concepts are distinct and, when properly implemented, corporate governance is a driver of efficiency, not red tape.[10]

It's moments like these that make the role of a company secretary both hilarious and stressful. Every day brings a new adventure, and sometimes, the stories are so unbelievable you couldn't make them up if you tried.

When done right, these inevitable challenges are managed with grace, professionalism, and efficiency, and resolved swiftly and smoothly. But on the flip side, the decisions made – whether good, bad, or ugly – can have a tangible impact on employees, owners and other stakeholders' day-to-day lives, significantly influence the company's profits and revenue, and affect its reputation and brand.

LEADERSHIP LESSON
Corporate failure rarely stems from one dramatic event – it's the result of small oversights, unchecked risks, and poor decisions left unchallenged.
Strong governance acts as the early warning system and stabilising force, quietly steering the organisation away from crisis and ensuring accountability before issues escalate beyond repair.

Company secretaries can be the unsung heroes of the organisation, saving more than just the day – sometimes, they avert a corporate scandal. While the job can have its lighter moments, its serious legal responsibilities are undeniable.

42% of corporate fraud cases result from a lack of internal controls, while another 29% are due to override of existing controls.[11]

A tale that would make anyone chuckle, if it were not for GDPR and all those pesky privacy rules. I would have loved to have kept the letter – it would be the crown jewel of hilarious mishaps.

Picture this: an old lady, Mrs Smiley, was perusing the newspaper aisle, minding her own business. Meanwhile a famous cracker company who make savoury snacks that look like miniature tree branches and have a tangy yeast extract flavour embarked on some mascot marketing: they had hired a gentleman to dress up as a giant mascot version of their 5cm 'stick like snack'. You can imagine the sight – a seven-foot stick waddling around the store!

The mascot, clearly taking some creative liberties with his role, decided it would be hilarious to hop into Mrs Smiley's trolley while she wasn't looking. So, there she was, turning back around to continue shopping, only to find this enormous mascot casually sitting in her trolley, legs crossed, reading a newspaper.

The poor woman was so shocked that she passed out on the spot, whacking her head as she went down. Naturally, she had to be taken to the hospital and spent the next three days recovering.

The first I heard of it was when I received a letter from her lawyer detailing the incident. It was so bizarre to read a legalistic letter setting out the incident – initially I wasn't sure if it was a joke!
Fortunately, we didn't have any legal pushback from the famous cracker company, who quietly settled the compensation costs with Mrs Smiley. As for the mascot, I'd like to think he's since retired from trolleys and taken up something less dramatic – like handing out samples. It's one of those moments that lives on in corporate folklore: part comedy sketch, part cautionary tale, and a reminder that no amount of brand marketing is worth a customer fainting in aisle three!

c.75% of company secretaries in the UK have a degree-level education in either law, business, finance, or related fields, these are commonly seen as essential for the role, alongside the professional postgraduate certification.[12]

And just when I thought I'd seen it all, along came a new CEO with a flair for the theatrical. His big idea? Our retailer should host a branded pop concert. Naturally, this involved flying in a world-renowned Italian opera singer – celebrated for his powerful tenor and equally powerful demands. He required two adjoining suites in a five-star London hotel: one shrouded in total darkness, the other containing only a grand piano for uninterrupted rehearsal.

It was a logistical circus, and my team and I were somehow expected to juggle it all. None of this fell under the company secretary remit, of course – but in roles like ours, adaptability is as essential as statute. Looking back, it was one of those moments that felt almost out of body. I remember thinking: is this governance?

When crisis strikes… call the company secretary

A company secretary becomes an even more valuable role to an organisation in a crisis. So, when the pandemic hit in March 2020, the CEO set up a 'war room' with key people on video calls three times a week. These calls involved managing business-critical decision-making, tracking the number of employees affected by the pandemic, and assessing the financial impact. When so many were navigating immense personal loss and uncertainty, our role in governance took on a different kind of weight. We weren't just grappling with legal compliance – we were helping leaders navigate a world that had suddenly shifted under everyone's feet.

We had to make critical decisions about how to sustain the business if the pandemic continued. My technical knowledge and experience were invaluable as we evaluated options like halting dividend payments to shareholders and adjusting share plans to conserve cash. We explored ways to save money for the greater good of the company and its employees, focusing on reward, retention, and well-being.

It's vital to come at these challenges with humanity, as whatever the outcome, the way these messages are delivered is so important in maintaining trust and respect. Adapting to this unprecedented situation required constant flexibility and quick thinking, and those discussions were instrumental in navigating the challenges the organisation faced during the pandemic.

It's now the norm to work remotely, but at the time, there was so much to wrestle with. Another significant aspect of my role was reviewing all the government guidelines. Unless you read them, you wouldn't realise how many were issued, detailing what we must and mustn't do. They were often conflicting, making it challenging to interpret what was permissible.

The biggest challenge for the directors was figuring out how to maintain normal activities, like staying at a hotel to attend multi-day board meetings. We found a solution with an exemption for staff canteens and in-house catering, so we had food delivered to the office. My team and I had to get creative to ensure our board meetings remained effective. We arranged socially distanced, in-person sessions, which allowed for much more natural and productive discussions compared to the awkward silence of virtual meetings.

Our role became even more crucial in managing the dynamic to ensure directors were set up to make the right decisions. It wasn't just about logistics; it was about creating the right environment – providing them with the right information at the right time, and ensuring they were in the right frame of mind to process it. After all, we're all human, and so are they. We had to think beyond the data, considering how emotions, reactions, and the atmosphere could impact the decisions being made. It was about striking a balance between the big picture and the subtle nuances that ultimately drive the best outcomes.

LEADERSHIP LESSON

Good governance goes beyond structure and compliance; it enables sound decision-making. That means curating not just the right information, but the right environment. Governance leaders anticipate emotional dynamics, manage timing, and foster clarity, they empower boards to act wisely and in the organisation's best interest.

Uniquely prepared for anything

Governance impacts every aspect of an organisation, making it a role that couldn't be furloughed during the pandemic. As this role is accountable to both the board, with executives working office hours, and non-executives often working outside office hours, it's easy to end up working around the clock.

A perplexing issue I've encountered in my career is the dual-hatted role of general counsel and company secretary. Merging these roles is complex because they require different post-graduate qualifications and distinct advisory responses based on the role being performed.

When the general counsel and company secretary roles are combined, it often leads to conflicting priorities. As general counsel, the focus is on protecting the legal interests of the company – handling litigation, compliance, contracts, and regulatory issues. In contrast, the company secretary's role centres on corporate governance, ensuring that the board and wider organisation operates within a structured framework of accountability and transparency.

These demands can often pull the individual in two opposing directions, making it difficult to provide clear, objective advice without inadvertently favouring one role over the other.

Moreover, this dual-hatted arrangement can create significant pressure on decision-making. The general counsel may prioritise minimising legal risk, while the company secretary might advocate for more open disclosures and greater board engagement.

This internal conflict can dilute the effectiveness of both roles, leaving the individual stretched thin and potentially exposing the company to vulnerabilities. Ideally, these roles would be held by two different, well-trained individuals with experience in their respective areas, but this is not always the case.

The company secretary job description can change dramatically, and CEOs can be particular about the type of person they want as their group company secretary since this person interacts with the board and often uncovers many of the organisation's darkest secrets.

Often, when a new company secretary is brought in, there's a realisation that the previous service level was inadequate. If you're good, CEOs frequently express surprise at the breadth of the role, saying they didn't realise the full extent of responsibilities beyond just minuting meetings.

Replacing a great company secretary is however challenging, much like replacing a CEO. The role is infused with personal traits, creativity, and values, making straightforward replacements impossible.

A good company secretary learns to think like a CEO, a Non-Executive Director (NED), and the chair as well as the other internal roles it interacts with. You have to really understand each of their personalities, skills, and approaches. Anticipating their questions is crucial, and it's frustrating when even 1% of their queries catch you off guard. Staying several steps ahead is key.

Each new board member too brings a unique dynamic, and I've often found new CEOs can require very different levels of support as they learn their role. Building a rapport with a new CEO can be slow, often necessitating more regular meetings to ensure visibility and avoid being forgotten.

It's common to have to explain to executive assistants why frequent meetings with the CEO are necessary, but it's vital, as you're often conveying important information from the chair, other directors, stakeholders or the organisation to prevent the CEO from being blindsided.

To be recognised in this role, you need to create significant value during engagements. Initially, it can be disheartening when people don't naturally think to involve the company secretary, but persistence and demonstrating value over time helps overcome these challenges. Directors, too, must recognise that building a strong relationship with their company secretary is in their best interest.

A proactive company secretary not only ensures smooth governance but can also anticipate potential risks and provide invaluable insights. When directors actively seek out and engage their company secretary, they gain a trusted adviser who can enhance decision-making and safeguard the organisation's long-term success.

Working in private equity was a whirlwind because decisions were made at lightning speed. With all the key decision-makers, including shareholders, present at every board meeting, there was no room for delay or deception. We could get fully endorsed decisions instantly.
I'd come out of a board meeting at 5pm and dive straight into action, often dealing with time-critical tasks like selling a business or acquiring another. We were dealing with transactions involving hundreds of millions – sometimes billions – of pounds, where a single misstep could have devastating consequences for the company's future and the livelihoods of everyone connected to it; the stakes were incredibly high.
Sometimes, we'd buy debt at a heavily discounted rate – say, 50p for every pound owed – because we were confident that the full amount would eventually be repaid. This strategy allowed us to acquire the debt for far less than its actual value, with the expectation of receiving a significant profit when the debtor settled the full amount.

It's a common practice in financial markets, particularly when dealing with distressed or undervalued debt, where we assess the risks and potential rewards before making such investments. The buyer takes on the risk that the debt may never be fully repaid, but if it is, they stand to profit. This practice is grounded in mutual agreement and market efficiency, where transparency and fairness are key. If the debtor is treated ethically and all parties understand the terms, buying debt at a discount can benefit everyone involved as it did for us.

In private equity opportunities are seized quickly, a dynamic that's impossible in the slower, more regulated listed world. You have instant feedback on whether decisions are being taken in the best long-term interest of the shareholders and stakeholders including your employees, customers and the community.

You've got one at the table who says yes, and, you know straight away; that's very powerful. This type of board structure allows for fast, strategic moves that maximise value and capitalise on undervalued assets. It's all about being in the right place, with the right knowledge, and acting quickly. However, if private equity drives a business purely for short-term gains, without considering the long-term impact, it can lead the company in the wrong direction, sacrificing sustainable growth and damaging both the brand and employee morale.

LEADERSHIP LESSON
Private equity brings agility – decisions are fast, direct, and often transformational. But speed must be balanced with stewardship. Effective governance in this space means leveraging the power of decisive action while maintaining a long-term lens.

Culture, ethics and DNA

When I joined one company, I quickly realised it was unique, driven by purpose and filled with great people. We didn't call our principles "values"; we refer to them as our DNA. One of my crucial responsibilities was ensuring new board members understood and embodied our DNA. During an induction for a new NED, I emphasised that these words might seem like marketing fluff, but each one has been meticulously crafted and debated by our executive team. "They truly represent us," I said. This fully embedded set of values drove our consistent double-digit growth and these values, and our culture was a key element of good governance.

Ensuring new board members internalise and practise our DNA isn't just corporate formality; it's critical for maintaining our blueprint for sustained success. As a key figure in this process, I bridge the gap between our foundational principles and their practical application, ensuring our culture remains robust and our growth, relentless.

Positive company culture can lead to a 33% increase in profits, while a good manager can result in a 27% higher revenue per employee[13]

Every time there's a new senior hire; my calendar fills up. Whether it's a new board member, CEO, chair, non-executive director, executive team member, or new key external adviser like auditors, lawyers, brokers, or head-hunters, I meet them all. My role is a constant amidst the sea of change. People come and go, roles evolve, and the company reshapes itself, but the core purpose generally remains steady.

It's a low-ego role, requiring authenticity. Even we struggle with it sometimes because, despite our purpose-driven mission, we still need to grow profits for our shareholders. We can't just say, "Here's your consistent profit, anything extra goes to charity." Shareholders expect continual growth, and that pressure is ever-present. It's often a given that as a company secretary you must often put on a "stiff upper-lip" and crack on with the job – as a soldier, not a commander – when the reality is that at times the workload can be overwhelming and has the potential to have a real impact on mental health and unsettle work–life balance.

In 2024:

- *31% of UK employees felt that they do not have a good work–life balance.*[14]
- *88% of UK employees have experienced burnout in the last two years.*[15]
- *UK employees work the longest hours in Europe with an average of 42 hours per week.*[16]

Shareholder engagement is also fascinating and, at times, hypocritical. Investment fund managers, who are on multimillion-pound salaries, often criticise CEOs' compensation packages. Yet, if a CEO resigns, the share price could plummet, wiping out millions in stock value.

There's a reason for their pay – it's tied to the high stakes and the immense responsibility of being a custodian of the company's assets. Being a CEO is also a 24/7, highly public role. It's demanding and scrutinised, but it's crucial. My job is to ensure every new hire understands this, maintaining our company's integrity and driving us forward amidst constant evolution.

> **LEADERSHIP LESSON**
> Criticism of executive pay can overlook the weight of responsibility. True governance ensures leaders are held accountable – and appropriately empowered – to protect long-term value in a high-stakes, high-scrutiny environment.

Impacting the bottom line

One of my most impactful projects involved overseeing our company's pension plan. When I started, I had to quickly learn the ropes, since I became the company-nominated trustee. My background in private equity and interest in investments helped, but this was a new challenge.

Handling the pension fund was more than just dry, administrative work. It involved making crucial investment decisions, sometimes dealing with multimillion-pound funds. We worked to close a significant £120 million deficit over three years.

By making strategic investment decisions and de-risking our portfolio, we turned a potential financial burden into a manageable situation. Making decisions as a board on selling a portion of our equity holdings and moving to bonds and gilts was a key part of that.

A memorable moment came during the chaotic aftermath of the October mini budget in 2022 under prime minister Liz Truss. It caused market turmoil, but it also reduced our pension deficit almost overnight. We had to act fast, something atypical in the pension world.

Throughout this project, it was my role to explain complex financial concepts to the board, ensuring they understood the risks and strategies. This proactive approach was crucial. By keeping a steady hand and leveraging my financial acumen, I helped navigate the company through turbulent times and secure the future of our pension plan.

There was a time when the pension fund was running low on cash reserves awaiting the sale of real estate. This is a typical scenario in the pension and savings world. We had c.£1 million left, which is fascinating to watch unfold.

However, amidst the chaos, opportunities often arise. In our case gilt rates hit 4% – a rare spike in 30 years. By understanding that a rise in gilt rates means a drop in gilt values, we could buy assets at a significant discount, then benefit as rates normalised.

Having such a deep involvement in this technical area allowed me to challenge investors and advisers effectively. They can't pull the wool over my eyes anymore, because I know the right questions to ask.

During the pandemic, we managed to freeze some of the company's contributions to the pension plan. The CEO remarked that this move could add £40 million to our market cap over the next five years, thanks to the cash savings.

This success was all about building and maintaining trust. The trustees know I wouldn't act solely in the company's interest, fostering a relationship where they feel comfortable challenging and consulting me directly. It's crucial, too, to recognise your limits and ensure you're covering all bases, even when you're confident in your approach.

Never stop learning

On-the-job training is invaluable, especially when you get the chance to learn directly from those who've been through these challenges and come out the other side with hard-earned wisdom. Sure, if you work in a regulated organisation, you might have the regulator mandating that you complete a foundational training course, which is good for the basics. But after that, it's all about inquiry and experience.

The best company secretaries I know don't just stop at formal training. They take the initiative to sit down with the group financial controller and ask tons of questions. They dive deep into what's being done, really getting to grips with the details. They aren't being annoying; they're being thorough. They look at everything put in front of them and test it, asking, "Is this right? How could this go wrong? Do we really mean this?" It's through this hands-on, inquisitive approach that you truly learn and excel.

Another role that required inquisitive thinking is that of the non-executive directors. They often say they're "coming in to kick the tires", which I've heard countless times, especially from the Audit Committee Chair. I've seen 'kicking the tires' then walking away – that's just irritating, and akin to criminal damage! But then there's the meaningful approach, where they prod a bit deeper, check the treads, and make sense of what's happening.

Every director should grasp the importance of their questions. It's about asking the right ones to get comfortable with the situation. As a trustee director, it's a huge responsibility, similar to being on the board. We're dealing with £300 million of pension money – people's future pensions – so every decision has to secure that.

Being insured helps; I'm not so worried about ending up in prison… but honesty is key. You need to maintain your integrity through everything and constantly question whether this is being obstructed by whomever is asking you to do something. You must be cautious and deliberate, because you're managing something critical and standalone: the governance of the organisation which affects every person who works with, works for, lives in the vicinity of or buys from it.

In this role, structuring things the right way and challenging experts can benefit everyone. I do this almost weekly. For example, just this morning, a global consulting firm rewrote its terms with a big US broker based on my feedback. Initially, they said the contract couldn't be changed as it was standard across clients. But by my asking, "How does this work?" they ended up rewriting the whole thing.

The lesson? Don't be afraid to challenge the unchallengeable. Pick your battles carefully and look for value. If you're dealing with a contract that's been in negotiation for months and suddenly needs signing in 24 hours, prioritise what's most important. Focus on the key change, like capping liability, rather than minor details. That's where you can make a real impact.

I've had the chance to work alongside some prominent business figures and observe them up close. One director in particular stood out – a brilliant mind, completely consumed by work. The kind of person who, quite honestly, might never stop working. He moved in powerful circles, with personal connections to senior politicians and well-known celebrities. His access was extraordinary.

Then there was someone I'll simply refer to as "the CEO" – a larger-than-life figure who eventually resigned over a scandal involving inappropriate conduct. He once turned up at our offices around Christmas, but fortunately, I managed to steer clear of any awkward moments. It wasn't unusual for unexpected guests to pop by; you never quite knew who you'd bump into next.

LEADERSHIP LESSON:
Working alongside high-profile, high-performing directors and senior executives offers insight – but also a reminder that brilliance and influence don't always equal integrity. The most effective governance leaders learn to ask the right questions, challenge when needed, and stay grounded in values, not personalities.

And here it ends...

Meeting interesting people is just part of the job, but it made me realise something key about being a company secretary. You've got to be human, be honest and treat people well. We're not in the limelight, but we're great at sharing knowledge and helping others rise.

In a well-designed team, it's not a dog-eat-dog world. It's all about supporting each other and growing together. The life of a company secretary isn't just a box of chocolates; it's also like riding a rollercoaster blindfolded whilst trying to keep those chocolates in place so you have a chance to pick your career path!

Reflecting on my career, I can't help but laugh — and sometimes cry — at the sheer unpredictability of it all. Yes, it's demanding and occasionally feels like navigating a minefield, but that's what makes it so incredibly rewarding.

No two days are ever the same, and that's exactly why I love what I do. The challenges are immense, but the stories? Absolutely priceless.

LEADERSHIP LESSON:
Great governance isn't about status – it's about service. The Company Secretary thrives not in the spotlight, but in the strength of relationships, quiet leadership, and a deep commitment to helping others succeed amidst the chaos.

CHAPTER 3

CHAPTER 3

CHAOS, CONTROL AND CREDIBILITY

Today was the same as yesterday – the Chair started piling tasks on my desk the moment I got in the office. I often say to myself, "for goodness sake, who put the Chair in charge of my sanity?" Like most chairs, he has a knack for wanting everything done in a particular way, at a particular time, with a particular flair. I don't think people realise just how much time company secretaries spend on the weirdest things! One minute you're handling a minor detail, and the next it's a colossal issue nobody saw coming.

LEADERSHIP LESSON
Staying grounded amidst shifting priorities requires resilience and that often lies in finding humour, patience, and perspective in the everyday chaos.

But let me backtrack a bit. I studied for a degree in law and politics which saw me heading to northern England with the ambition to become a solicitor. This decision was motivated by the allure of a corporate career. During my studies, I strategically selected modules to keep my career options flexible.

Approximately 65% of company secretaries in FTSE 100 companies are lawyers, either in combined or standalone roles.[17]

At the whim of others

As I explored my career options, I encountered the qualification to become a Chartered Governance Professional, which offered a direct route to senior roles within corporate governance. This alternative promised a blend of legal, managerial and administrative responsibilities, aligning well with my aspirations.

Despite my legal training, I quickly realised that a career as a solicitor was not the right fit for me. Visits to several law firms reinforced this conclusion. The prospect of engaging directly with board-level activities without the intense competition of the legal profession was particularly appealing.

Upon graduation, it took me a few months scanning invoices before I was spotted and secured my first trainee role with an overseas-headquartered oil and gas company. I was based in the UK satellite office and managed its operations in regions such as Nigeria and Yemen, with board meetings held in Jersey. As the guardian of corporate governance, I was given the authority and independence to advise the board objectively. The private office I received from the outset recognised the critical influence and advisory role even a Trainee company secretary holds within an organisation.

The company secretarial path has both proved to be engaging and allowed me to thrive in a dynamic and more humanistic role than that of a corporate lawyer. When it comes to the company you work for, it's about finding the right fit: the company's culture, ethics, and the product or service they offer need to resonate with your values and interests, as you're at the heart of ensuring its leadership works efficiently and effectively. In order to make a real difference it's vital to truly understand everything about the organisation you work for and be passionate about it.

When I moved on from my trainee position, I landed a job with the perfect culture fit, where I worked under two phenomenal female bosses; they were astonishing, and I learned so much from them. The value I gained from that one role was immense; they entrusted me with significant duties and allowed me to represent the company and share its views on corporate responsibility at an industry forum, even though I was still early in my career.

I was responsible for ghost writing on behalf of the CEO, CFO and Chair of the Board. My responsibility extended to the text at the front of the annual financial statements that sets out the company's vision, mission and accomplishments to date. The sort of thing that would be an opening address for these individuals at an investor presentation. I worked with designers to create this important investor document, ensuring it was 'on brand' in terms of look and feel, and collaborated with consultants and colleagues to draft the content of more than fifty pages on company strategy, governance and future plans.

LEADERSHIP LESSON

Success isn't always about following the path you first trained for – it's about recognising where your strengths, values, and passions truly align. The most meaningful leadership journeys begin when you find a role and culture that challenges you and nurtures your potential.

I am the one and only!

Changing jobs for anyone means navigating new managers, a brand-new culture and lots of upheaval. But changing roles as a company secretary means much more tumult than a typical job (more like that of a CEO) – it means that you have to relearn everything you know about how you operate. Governance requires some creativity – it's not a set of hard and fast rules, it's a set of principles.

Like an artist needs to understand the client's vision, so a governance professional needs to understand what the governance 'tastes' are in a new organisation. The openness of leadership to change what has 'always been done that way' is important too, as sometimes processes, procedures or approaches may have run their course, or have never been the right fit for the company from the start.

Doctor Google is not your friend

Don't get me started on googling 'governance' and just adopting what looks good or creating a carbon copy of what others do – you need the right governance for your organisation. You wouldn't adopt this paint-by-numbers approach with company strategy, so why would you do it for the structure that fits around that strategy, builds the culture, and creates efficient and ethical ways of working?

The constant struggle to get people to understand what we do and why it matters is huge but could have serious consequences. It's not just about proclaiming, "We're governance professionals and governance is great!" because, let's be honest, that line doesn't carry much weight. Despite the complexity and importance of governance, it's often seen as just pushing papers and writing minutes. But it's so much more than that. It's about ensuring that everything is done correctly, legally and ethically across the organisation; it informs everyone's work in the organisation, either in the way they do it or the way they conduct themselves.

Some CEOs, CFOs and Chairs still need to get on board and understand the benefits good governance will have on achieving their goals! It's mind blowing that these tools at their disposal are being left underutilised or, at worst, ignored.

In the UK, corporate failures have steadily increased in the past few decades, with some estimates showing that on average over 300,000 businesses fail annually.[18]

I vividly remember one instance that truly tested my limits. We were in the middle of a massive project to do capital reductions for subsidiaries – essentially, moving cash out of certain companies to prepare clean balance sheets for dissolution. The project manager, who wasn't in Company Secretarial, realised at the eleventh hour that the work needed to be done, and I found myself spending the entire weekend buried in paperwork. There were literally hundreds of documents to draft and minutes to prepare. A detailed step-by-step plan had been written, but no one had thought to check in with the governance team until we were actioning that step. Navigating these last-minute curveballs was exhausting.

The failure to check in with the governance team didn't just cost me a weekend of work, we also ended up spending c.£12,000 on external legal fees to fix some of the oversights that, had I been given early sight of the plan, would not have occurred. When these things happen there's always that little voice of guilt wondering, *Should I have known about this project and stepped in earlier?*

Fixing the problem could also have fallen to me, but when it comes down to the technicalities of legal compliance when things have already gone wrong publicly, sometimes you have to set aside your pride and bring in the experts, because getting it right matters more than anything.

The World Economic Forum's Global Risks Report 2023 emphasises that major crises, including corporate failures, are increasingly driven by systemic risks such as poor governance, financial mismanagement, and economic shocks.[19]

I'll politely decline, thank you

The funny thing is, even though we're the experts on listing rules and governance, people still sometimes think we need help with the most basic things. I have had some bizarre requests from our corporate legal team, who, quite honestly, don't have much experience when it comes to the intricacies of the corporate world from a listing perspective. People often suggest I check with corporate legal, and I'm like, no thanks, they don't understand governance – you wouldn't check with a brain surgeon if you needed advice on a broken bone, similarly, I won't get the advice I need from legal on governance issues. If I really want the right guidance, I'll go external. It's almost as if people don't truly understand what we do or the depth of our role.

The UK was the world 'founding father' of Corporate Governance and its "comply or explain" approach in 1992, following the Cadbury Report.[20]

Case in point: this week, our major shareholder comes to me asking what he needs to do under the DTRs (the Financial Conduct Authority's Disclosure and Transparency Rules). First off, I'm not comfortable advising any of our investors on what they should be doing under the DTRs – they need to get their own advice. Second, what a cheek! Instead of paying for his own legal counsel, he's trying to get it from us. So naturally, I turn to our general counsel explaining my views – except here's the problem: they don't have a background with listed companies. And guess what? They go and ask the CFO and the Head of Investor Relations what to say in reply to me. Meanwhile, I'm thinking, neither of them are experts on listing rules, so it's back to me.

In the end I shared my initial thoughts with the CFO etc but said, just to be safe, we should confirm externally. You trust your gut, but when the stakes are high, it's worth a quick call to the brokers or external governance advisers to make sure you're covered – especially when you're dealing with a shareholder who could turn hostile.

In the end, everyone agreed with my approach, but it made me realise how much we still battle against the perception that our outputs always need to be checked with someone 'cleverer'. Even the general counsel didn't seem to know that *I* am the expert on listing rules! It's that constant struggle – people still see us as administrative support rather than a source of real expertise.

Sometimes, it feels like we're still expected to do things as trivial as coffee runs, and it's frustrating. Sure, we'll help, but there's a cost to being overly helpful. By taking on these small tasks, we're chipping away at the real value we bring to the table, and that's part of the challenge we face every day.

Working as a company secretary is living a double life – one moment you're making high-level decisions on multimillion-pound transactions, the next you're sourcing a meeting room in London with an impossible list of demands.

No one told me I'd be doing things like signing contracts for dogs starring in TV shows, or ensuring the director with a pacemaker doesn't keel over at the AGM because of a magnetic name badge. But that's the reality.

LEADERSHIP LESSON

Leadership means knowing the value of your expertise – even when others don't. Just because someone holds authority doesn't mean they hold the right answer; credibility comes from understanding where true insight lives.

Shh… no one's supposed to know about this yet!

Our role is in the trenches, navigating the extremes of governance, law, and the human element that connects everything. It's not just about knowing the rules – it's about understanding the nuance of when a seemingly insignificant detail, like a shareholder's sudden desire to go rogue, could blow up into something that affects the entire company. And, trust me, when you're the one making sure the Chair's hush-hush meetings stay hush-hush, or handling board egos, it's hard to explain to anyone outside the circle just how much is at stake.

70-90% of mergers and acquisitions fail, often due to poor integration, misaligned strategies, and cultural clashes.[21]

As a Company Secretary, maintaining composure is crucial. The moment you appear panicked, you risk signalling to everyone that something business-critical is unravelling, which can cause unnecessary alarm and speculation. But beyond that, visibly losing your cool diminishes the respect and confidence the board of directors have in you.

Your role is to be the steady hand guiding the ship through complex governance, legal, and compliance waters, and if you falter, it not only undermines your authority but also weakens your ability to manage the board effectively. Staying calm under pressure isn't just about appearances; it's about preserving trust and demonstrating leadership in moments that matter most.

Building a relationship of trust with someone at a leadership level typically takes six months to a year or more.[22]

In one job I was an outlier in a bubble of luxury fashion, while the finance team questioned why we weren't handling every little legal task ourselves. "Why do we need the external advisers?" they'd ask. What they didn't grasp was what was at stake in that moment and that one wrong move could cost the company millions, but also, more painfully for me, could cost me my job! And let's not forget, in this workplace everyone was judged as much by how well they fit in with the luxury fashion aesthetic; we were selling alligator-skin trench coats for £72,000.

I didn't fit the typical mould, but I focused on doing the work well. Over time, that spoke louder than anything else.

In this line of work, it's not about shouting from the rooftops about governance. It's about proving, time and time again, that we're the ones who hold it all together when things threaten to fall apart. And still, no one outside this role ever truly knows the magnitude of the challenges we face.

LEADERSHIP LESSON

In high-stakes environments, your calm is your credibility. True leadership is measured not by how loudly you act, but by how steadily you lead when the pressure peaks.

The boss is coming, look busy

When I joined one of the UK's leading FTSE-listed broadcasting giants, I knew I was stepping into a mess. The team was running on fumes – every Friday they were churning out pointless work-in-progress reports instead of actually getting the work done. It was classic corporate bureaucracy, more about looking productive than *being* productive.

For six months, I was part firefighter, part therapist – calming the team down, ditching the meaningless tasks and meetings, and focusing on what we were really supposed to be doing. It was untangling a knot of chaos and trying to restore some sanity to the system.

70% of meetings are deemed unproductive by employees.[23]
#itcouldhavebeenanemail

Bully-boy tactics

The real challenge wasn't just the workload – it was navigating the egos and power plays at the top. One of the most difficult people I worked with went on to become an MP, which still surprises me to this day.

This guy was a bully, plain and simple. He thrived on intimidation, and the worst part was watching how the CEO enabled him. The CEO had been promoted up through the ranks multiple times, not because of merit, but because he was a classic 'yes-man'. He never challenged the status quo, never pushed back – and that's exactly what they wanted. It's surprisingly common – I'm sure this approach rings loudly in everyone's ears, given recent corporate scandals where inept senior people tried to 'play CEO'. What struck me the most was how disconnected the CEO was from the chair, almost like he wasn't supposed to have a close relationship with him. It didn't sit right with me.

I watched these dynamics and all I could think was how wrong it was. Letting it play out wasn't just about keeping the peace – it was about keeping my seat at the table so I could make a difference when it mattered most. It is when you can see the bigger picture and others cannot that you need to use your access to the boardroom to help mitigate a disaster.

Governance professionals should be in the thick of it, shaping decisions, building relationships, and holding people accountable and, on occasion, with the ear of the board, calling out the absurdities of certain decisions like an internal whistleblower – after all, our role is to be the conscience of the company. It's scary to see how easy it can be for people to mould a 'yes-man' into their puppet, and it only made me more determined to fight for the integrity and independence of my role.

The miracle-workers

If a board is a dysfunctional family, then the Executive Assistants (EAs) are the unsung heroes. Imagine a group of highly skilled individuals, wildly diverse in their personalities, backgrounds, and quirks, yet thrust into the role of wrangling executives and smoothing over the chaos behind the scenes. They've got their own internal politics too, mind you. You'll often find them with unresolved issues, petty rivalries, or sometimes just an unspoken competition to outdo each other. Yet, despite these seemingly random conflicts with other EAs, they are nothing short of brilliant.

These EAs work tirelessly, navigating the daily storm of corporate dysfunction with the finesse of seasoned diplomats. They are the gatekeepers, the fixers, the miracle-workers. And they do it all while managing the personal dramas of their executives – late-night emails, last-minute flight changes, temperamental personalities, and even the occasional executive meltdown.

LEADERSHIP LESSON

Real leadership isn't about keeping power players happy – it's about having the courage to challenge dysfunction and protect the integrity of the organisation. When influence is abused and accountability ignored, the true leaders are those who speak truth to power and use their access not for favour, but for impact.

Geek to the rescue

It was the usual end-of-meeting shuffle – directors gathering their papers, exchanging handshakes, half out the door in their minds, already thinking about their next meeting or a quick lunch. That's often when my moment came. Not with grand gestures or a raised voice, but with a calm interruption – the kind that cuts through the room without needing to shout. I leaned in slightly, just enough to signal I wasn't quite finished. "By the way," I said, projecting clearly but keeping the tone steady, "just to remind everyone – this now counts as inside information. So no buying or selling shares."

That's what it meant to be the gatekeeper. While others packed up, I stayed rooted in the role that makes governance work in practice – the person who names the thing no one else is thinking about until it's too late.

The Chair, one of the old hands on the board, turned to me with a smirk. "Ah, there we go," he chuckled, "the governance nerds swoop in to keep us in line." There was a wryness in his voice – part joke, part respect. He didn't mean it unkindly, and we both knew it. Beneath the remark was an unspoken understanding: this wasn't about red tape or ticking boxes. It was about protecting the integrity of the company – especially in the moments when no one else remembered to.

In those moments, you realise how vital the role of company secretary truly is. We don't just handle the paperwork or make sure the i's are dotted and t's are crossed. We're the checks and balances, the steady hands that guide the ship. And there's always one or two directors – like that Chair – who get it. They might joke, but deep down, they understand that we're the ones ensuring that decisions are being made not just with the company's financial interests in mind, but with its ethical standing intact.

It's my way or the highway

When I first stepped into the role, there was some discussion about reporting lines – not just about responsibilities, but structure. Should I report directly to the chair of the board, or to the CEO? In the end, it was agreed that I'd report to the CEO, which made sense operationally. What mattered more was maintaining the right level of independence. I didn't need to be in lockstep with the CEO, nor best mates. Our roles serve different purposes, and at times, our priorities naturally diverged. And that was not only expected – it was necessary.

The chair, though? That was a different dynamic altogether. I used to joke he was a bit like the Eye of Sauron from *Lord of the Rings* – always scanning, always watching, ready to zero in the moment something didn't look quite right. It wasn't paranoia; it was precision. And in his own way, he kept everyone on their toes – myself included. But being a first-time chair, he still had the itch of an executive, wanting to dip his toe into everything operational, a big governance no-no.

The trick was keeping the unnecessary stuff off his radar, letting him focus on what truly mattered, while I managed the things that could be handled without his interference. To be fair, the CEO was surprisingly good at letting me get on with what I needed to do – most of the time. Except when it came to the executive committee meetings. Honestly, they were the bane of my existence. The CEO was relentless – he pored over every line, dissected every slide, and never missed a typo. "This paper's crap," he'd mutter, while I sat thinking, this is what your executive team put together. I could rewrite it, of course – but that's not my role.

My role is to guide, to offer advice on how to improve it, but there's only so much I can do. The real issue is that some of these executives couldn't communicate their strategy clearly if their life depended on it.

It was all data dumps and jargon, no clarity or insight. But that's the part that gets him most excited – digging through the data and getting riled up when he spots that the numbers don't tell a consistent message.

LEADERSHIP LESSON

Clarity of role is essential – leadership means understanding where your responsibilities begin and end, and resisting the pull to fix what others must own. Maintain independence, guide with integrity, and protect the boundaries that enable governance to function as it should.

A celebration cake for one

Of course, what you can't say in the boardroom is that the person who drafted that paper practically shrugged me off when I asked them to follow the template. Or that they claimed it'd take another week to revise and wasn't worth the effort. These are the behind-the-scenes skirmishes – the ones no one sees, and no one wants to hear about. You just find a way to make it work, quietly sidestepping landmines and keeping the show on the road.

What I've come to understand in this role is that doing the work isn't enough. You have to keep proving your value. Sometimes that means tactfully highlighting your wins – like the time I got a proxy adviser to reverse their recommendation and vote in our favour. For those unfamiliar, proxy advisers hold considerable sway in corporate governance. Their guidance can influence the outcome of critical shareholder votes in the Annual General Meeting (AGM) which could include director reappointments, remuneration etc – so if they advise against you, you've got a real battle on your hands.

Changing a proxy adviser's recommendation is no small feat. It takes a firm grasp of governance, negotiation, and corporate strategy to shift the view of people who rarely change their minds. You have to make a compelling case, answer every concern, and do it with precision – because the stakes at an AGM are high. When I managed to turn that vote around, it wasn't just a governance win; it protected the company's position. But if I hadn't flagged it, it would've flown under the radar. The CEO's "Well done" was polite enough – but it reminded me that these invisible wins often need to be made visible. They're proof of the strings we pull to keep the company steady, even when no one's watching.

Then there's our CFO...

As ESG (Environment, Social and Governance) reporting – which in this organisation sits with the Chief Financial Officer (CFO) – becomes more central, our paths cross more often. We have our regular catchups, but the relationship is still a bit formal. It's like pulling teeth to get him to see me as the expert in governance. In his mind, the general counsel – the top legal adviser to the company – still wears that mantle. And of course, the general counsel isn't about to say, "Oh no, that's not me – better talk to the company secretary."

More than 1,300 of the largest UK-registered companies have been mandated to report on ESG matters.[24]

You're constantly having to position yourself as the go-to on governance – even if it takes time to land. I just wish some general counsels would drop the "I know everything" attitude when it comes to governance and listing rules. In my experience, that kind of overconfidence has a way of backfiring – often quite publicly, and usually right in front of the full board.

If I can I'll gallantly step in and catch them before they make a blooper. Still, sometimes it's too far gone, and I sit there with a neutral, unsympathetic facial expression, trying to hide my satisfaction at the sight of him trying and failing to show he could do my job.

So how do you navigate these high-stakes games with so many overinflated egos? The key is to remain curious – being genuinely interested in what motivates people, why they do what they do, and where the pressure points are. A good sense of humour helps, too. Everyone has one, even if it's buried deep down. And then there's empathy, the ability to read a room and understand the unspoken dynamics at play. You might sense something's off, but figuring out how to address it strategically is a skill we continually hone over our careers.

Too big for my own boots

Ah yes, I've had my missteps. Once, I accused my boss, the CEO, of doing something wrong, only to find out later I was completely off base. He made me apologise, and there I was, feeling like a schoolkid being sent to the principal's office. But you learn from those moments.

The next time he came into the office, feeling stressed because he couldn't find his keys, I was able to calm him down with a light comment. I said, "Take a deep breath, we'll figure it out," and we both shared a smile. It's moments like these that help strengthen our working relationship and build the trust we rely on during more challenging situations.

98% of CEOs prefer job candidates with a sense of humour.[25]

In the end, it's not the flashy victories we celebrate. It's the fact that things didn't go wrong, that the press didn't pick up a news story, that the ship kept sailing smoothly through turbulent waters. That's the heart of what we do – making sure everything runs so seamlessly that no one even notices the fires we've put out behind the scenes, the headlines that don't get printed.

Stay in your lane and I'll stay in mine

There are conversations I simply can't have with the general counsel – and that's not a slight, it's just the nature of our distinct roles. In truth, many of the general counsels I've worked with don't know about the finer details of the listing rules or corporate governance – and that's entirely fair. Their strength lies elsewhere: in navigating contract law, regulatory frameworks, and litigation risk. That legal expertise is critical to protecting the organisation, and it gives governance professionals like me the space to focus on board effectiveness, regulatory compliance, and stakeholder alignment with full confidence that the legal foundations are secure.

Approximately 40% of the FTSE100 have combined roles of general counsel and company secretary, conversely.[26]

And that's fine by me, really. I've always been the one to bridge the gaps between groups. Seniority, hierarchy – it doesn't faze me. I talk to everyone, from the boardroom down to the operations team. If there's value in a relationship, I'll build on it, but I don't base my moves on titles. I know the value I bring – and when it comes to governance, particularly in listed environments, I lead from experience. Others may have different perspectives, but this is my lane, and I'm comfortable steering it.

LEADERSHIP LESSON
General counsels and company secretaries may work closely, but their roles are not interchangeable – one anchors legal risk, the other ensures governance integrity. True leadership recognises that effective collaboration comes from respecting these differences while aligning around a shared commitment to the organisation's success.

Writing everything down: Because memory is a terrible secretary

Imagine this: during a period of intense change, it's not uncommon as a company secretary to juggle around 120 board and board committee meetings in a single year. That's 200 days – nearly ten solid months – dedicated solely to prepping, attending, advising at and minuting the meetings, the only legal record of what happened that would ever be used in court. It can be a marathon of boardroom madness.

During one particular stretch, we had a rights issue, a placing, Brexit chaos that forced us into disenfranchisement decisions, a takeover approach – it felt like the universe was throwing everything at us at once.

"The minutes are what the board wished they had said, written by a secretary who spent hours making it sound that way." – Anon[27]

One of the most high-pressure moments of my career was overseeing a £500 million payout from a share scheme following a takeover. Every detail had to be flawless, funds in the right accounts, on time, with zero margin for error. The external providers were out of their depth, so I had to walk them through the process line by line until every scheme was watertight. In the end, we delivered it seamlessly.

The irony of the whole thing was that after all that meticulous planning and high-wire execution, no one even noticed. But that's the beauty of what we do. Our biggest victories are often the things that go unnoticed because nothing goes wrong. No major headlines, no PR disasters – just a very calm, "business as usual" appearance.

When we manage to pull off these colossal feats, and the press has nothing to write about, that's when we know we've done our job right. We celebrate the mundane, the quiet victories, the non-events. It's not glamorous, but it's the heart of what we do – making sure the business keeps moving forward without anyone ever realising how close we came to chaos. It's funny when you think about it: we're proudest when nothing happens.

In 2017, United Airlines forcibly removed a passenger from an overbooked flight, and viral videos of the bloodied man being dragged down the aisle sparked widespread outrage. Customers boycotted the airline, and its share price dropped over 4%, erasing nearly US$1 billion in market value.[28]

Tragedy and loss

There are moments in life that weigh so heavily on the heart, they leave an imprint that never truly fades. Moments when you carry a burden no one else knows about, all while the world around you continues, oblivious, as if nothing has changed. It's in those moments when the hardest thing you can do is smile.

Smile and nod as people talk excitedly about holiday plans, destinations they've dreamed of visiting while you carry the weight of what you know – that those bonuses they're counting on to make their plans come true... well, they're never going to materialise. And they don't know. They talk about flights they've booked, hotels they've researched, and you know that soon, it will all come crashing down for them.

It's a cruel twist of life to be the bearer of bad news. You're the one who holds the knowledge that a decision has been made, a restructuring is imminent, that jobs are about to be lost. You sit in meetings where people smile and talk about how well things are going, unaware that the conversation in the boardroom paints a far darker picture. You nod along, even as the dissonance tears at you inside. It's heartbreaking – your role demands that you withhold the truth, but your heart aches for the people who trust in a future that's slipping away before your eyes.

And then there was *John* (fictitious name). He stood apart – the kind of leader who wasn't just a name on the door or a face at the boardroom table. He was present, approachable, and deeply human. He'd already been with the company six years when I joined, and though I didn't know him in those early days, I came to know him well. *John* wasn't the sort of chair who stayed locked away in an office. He'd stop and chat with anyone, even by the photocopier.

He genuinely cared about the company, and during some of our toughest times – Brexit, the pandemic, the grounding of the fleet, and shareholder battles – *John* was a constant. Calm, smiling, and quietly resolute. After everything he gave, no one deserved retirement more than he did.

But life rarely gives us what we deserve. *John* stepped down from the board at the start of the month, ready to finally slow down after years of relentless dedication. Just days later, he passed away. A man who had weathered so much, who had earned his rest, was gone before he could begin to enjoy it. It didn't seem fair. Yes, he'd been unwell – but we all believed he'd recover. He was looking forward to the next chapter. And then, just like that, it ended.

We wanted to honour him in the end-of-year report. Nothing extravagant – just a simple tribute to someone who gave so much of himself to the company. But bureaucracy has a way of stripping the humanity out of moments like these. The auditors pushed back, citing legal risks and the implications of reopening the accounts. But to us, it wasn't about legality or liability. It was about doing what was right. We fought for that tribute – not because it made corporate sense, but because it was the right thing for *John*.

Life moves on, but moments like these leave you hollow. You're managing real, human grief while still keeping the business running. And sometimes, everything seems to go wrong at once – mistakes in the accounts, mounting pressure, that overwhelming sense of holding things together while everything's falling apart. These moments stay with you. They don't fade. You just learn to carry them, hoping they'll make sense in the long run. Sometimes they don't. And that's just life.

LEADERSHIP LESSON

Leadership sometimes means holding difficult information before others are ready to hear it, balancing transparency with discretion. It's not about grand gestures, but about showing empathy, maintaining trust, and doing what's right – even when it's hard and goes unnoticed.

A lesson learnt on the job

In my first senior role, I walked straight into a storm – one of those classic "oh no" moments that hits you like a freight train. We were about to issue new shares for a company share plan. Everything was moving… until someone realised, we didn't have a block listing in place. It was like planning a party and forgetting to book the venue.

Cue panic. I didn't even know what a block listing was at that point. I should have – but I didn't. So, I did what you do in a crisis: I picked up the phone. Our brokers talked me through it, step by step. First, we had to get the initial listing of the shares sorted. Then came the block listing, which would allow us to issue shares on an ongoing basis. But there was more – hedging discussions followed to manage exposure to market swings.

It was a crash course in corporate finance I didn't ask for, but it gave me more than any formal training ever could. At the time, it felt like a disaster. Now, I see it for what it was: one of the steepest, sharpest learning curves of my career.

Another time I was pulled into a crisis management test. The Executive Committee asked me to come along as the note-taker which, in theory, seemed like a simple task. But in reality, it was an absolute nightmare.

Imagine trying to jot down everything that's being discussed while, at the same time, everyone's turning to you and saying, "Do we agree on this?" I'm sitting there, barely keeping up, thinking, "Bloody hell, I'm just trying to track all the chaos!" That moment taught me something important – being the note-taker in a crisis is not where my strengths lie.

In a real crisis, the role isn't just to scribble down decisions. It's about being the calm in the storm. You have to step back and provide objectivity. You're the one who asks the tough questions: Do we notify the board yet? What about the investors or regulators? What are the real consequences here?

Only 50% of organisations have a crisis response plan and only 45% conduct regular risk audits.[29]

I've handled my share of crises, but nothing came close to the chaos when the pandemic hit. Overnight, we were looking at grounding the entire fleet. As if that wasn't enough, our largest shareholder launched a campaign to remove a board member which escalated to four people and they even threatened legal action, claiming we hadn't called a valid general meeting. It was relentless, and every day felt like a new fire to put out.

And then there was the cyberattack – another crisis that hit us hard. Each of these situations felt like the world was on fire, and my job was to connect the dots, to figure out how to keep things from collapsing.

But sometimes, it's the quieter crises that leave the biggest mark. Like the time we lost the vote for the remuneration report at the AGM on the very last day of the proxy voting. The morning vote showed 52% in favour, but by the afternoon it had flipped to 52% *against*. You're left explaining to directors why they're losing support with investors, sometimes even telling them it's time to step down. It's brutal, but it's part of the job. Every major storm I've weathered has taught me more about handling crisis than I could've ever imagined.

Celebrity endorsement

Working at a TV broadcaster came with some unexpected perks – the occasional celebrity sighting being one of them. I'd find myself in the lift next to Ant and Dec, heart racing just a little as I mumbled a polite "hi," trying to act like it was totally normal. It wasn't. Then there were moments when I couldn't resist asking for a selfie – like with Damien Lewis, who was surprisingly laid-back and even gave me advice on the best angle.

Helen Fielding looked genuinely shocked (and a bit delighted) that someone recognised her and was all smiles for the photo. I also crossed paths with James Morrison, James Bay, and Tinie Tempah – though in one selfie with him, all I could focus on was my double chin. These encounters were brief, but they added a little spark to the everyday, moments I didn't take for granted.

Anticipatory fear

In the world I work in, there's this constant undercurrent of anticipation – especially when it comes to disclosures. I mean, there's always that nagging worry: have we done the right thing here? You can talk to your advisers and try to get comfortable, but let's be real, sometimes you don't. And then comes that gut-punch moment, like, "Oh no, is the FCA going to come knocking with an investigation?" It's that creeping dread that sneaks in when you get notifications or letters about some looming investigation or issue.

1 in 5 people *in the UK workforce are experiencing moderate to severe anxiety, significantly impacting their job performance and overall well-being.*[30]

But here's the thing – and this is what experience has taught me – those moments that feel like the end of the world at the time? They're usually not. Sure, at the moment, it feels massive, like the sky is falling. But with time, you realise most of these crises are just part of the job.

I remember every time we'd get a lawyer's letter from our major shareholder's legal team "Oh no, what now?" The initial reaction was always panic, "What are we going to do with this one?" But after that moment passed, it was game on. Alright, let's fight this. Let's deal with it and move on." And somehow, every time, we did. What started as dread would eventually turn into a challenge to tackle head-on – and in the end, those challenges often led to positive outcomes.

LEADERSHIP LESSON

In high-stakes environments, anxiety is inevitable – but strong leaders know that most crises aren't catastrophes. Resilience means recognising the fear, then moving through it to find clarity, solutions, and often unexpected growth.

Survival and a small serving of PTSD

You know, looking back, I think I might still be carrying some PTSD from that whole experience. It's funny, isn't it? You think you've moved on, but every now and then something triggers a memory, and you realise that what you went through, what we all went through, left a deeper mark than you expected. The hours we worked, the sheer amount of effort and energy we poured into just getting through it – it was relentless. Six months of really intense work.

Every day felt like a battle, and I'm probably still recovering from that period. You didn't have a choice but to believe you were going to win. It wasn't just about optimism; it was about survival. We knew we were right. We knew what our major shareholder was doing was irrational, and that was the mindset that kept us going.

An estimated 875,000 UK workers suffer from work-related stress, depression, or anxiety, leading to 17.1 million working days lost.[31]

But it wasn't just about knowing we were right – it was about resilience. You had to keep pushing, even when it felt like there was no end in sight. Board meetings stacked up like dominoes, and each one felt like its own small war.

While everyone else seemed consumed by the chaos of the pandemic, we were so deep in our own crisis that we barely even registered what was happening with the rest of the world. The pandemic was just noise in the background, something we'd only get around to worrying about once we'd dealt with the immediate firestorm in front of us.

It wasn't until we wrapped things up mid-year, after the share placing, that I finally paused and realised – *oh wait, there's this pandemic thing everyone's talking about*. A month on and we were suddenly catching up with the world, almost like waking up from a long, strange dream. It's strange to think about now, but I suppose that's the power of sheer focus and determination.

There were moments when I wasn't sure how we'd keep going, but we did. And when it was finally over, the sense of relief was overwhelming. But the exhaustion? That stayed with me. Even now, I think back on it and realise just how much we had to endure, and how much it shaped who I am today. But that doesn't make it right; it was incredibly unhealthy.

LEADERSHIP LESSON

Resilience isn't about heroics – it's about staying grounded when things get tough. Real motivation comes from a quiet commitment to doing what's needed, not for praise, but because the work matters.

A nail-biting showdown

It was supposed to be just another job, the kind where you settle in for a while, find your rhythm, and maybe even build something long-term. But just six months in, the ground shifted beneath us. A takeover approach. One suitor made sense – I had half-expected them. But the second bidder? They came out of nowhere, blindsiding us with their offer. Suddenly, we were thrust into a high-stakes game.

The whole thing escalated into an auction – an intense, nail-biting showdown. Normally, these kinds of deals would drag out over five days, a slow burn of negotiation and counteroffers. But we didn't want that. We pushed to condense it into a single day, a Saturday, of all days. The office was empty except for us – a small group of advisers and decision-makers gathered in a quiet war room, plotting our moves with the precision of a chess game.

The tension was palpable. Each bid that came in sent a ripple through the room. We were watching the numbers climb, the stakes getting higher with every round. We had mapped out almost every possibility, but nothing could have prepared us for the final bid. Out of nowhere, the second bidder massively upped their offer, far surpassing the initial suitor's highest bid. The room fell silent for a moment as we processed what had just happened. It was shocking – no one had expected them to go that far.

I took a moment to look around the room and take it all in. We were in the middle of something historic, and the weight of it wasn't lost on me. I snapped a few photos – not for show, but to remind myself later that this really happened. The office was quiet, the lights dimmed, just a handful of us locked in, working through the night. No dramatic speeches, no cinematic flair – just focus, urgency, and the sense that we were right at the centre of something that mattered. It left its mark.

Of course, not every day in this role is filled with the adrenaline of billion-pound deals. There's a complexity to what we do that often goes unseen. It's not just about the legalities or the paperwork. It's about safeguarding the interests of the board, balancing strategy with governance, and navigating the grey areas where there are no clear answers. You have to understand the company inside and out; where management is headed, what the board needs, and what the investors expect. It's like threading a needle in a storm, with all of these forces pulling in different directions.

Lawyers are crucial, no doubt about that. But they don't handle the delicate dance of investor relations or feel the pulse of what's expected in terms of governance. That's where we come in. We're the ones who bridge the gap between the boardroom, management, and stakeholders, making sure everything aligns.

Sure, lawyers might get the spotlight, but let's not kid ourselves – it's often the company secretaries working behind the scenes who keep things running smoothly. We're the ones who handle the complex web of relationships and navigate the storm. In any other job, no one would take someone else's title and claim to do their work. So why should it be any different here?

In the end, it's not about getting the credit. It's about making sure everything holds together, even when things get rough. And trust me, I've been through my fair share of turbulence. But that Saturday auction? That was a storm I'll never forget.

The silent heroes

As I look back on the journey, I realise that the true value of what we do often goes unnoticed, and that's just fine by me. The companies I've been fortunate enough to work for, the teams I've been lucky enough to be a part of – it's all been a learning experience. Sure, there have been intense moments – takeovers, boardroom dramas, crises that felt like the world was collapsing – but through it all, one constant has remained: the camaraderie, the shared sense of purpose, and yes, the occasional laugh to lighten the load.

You go into this career thinking it's all about governance, regulations, and making sure the board's interests are protected – and it is, in many ways. But at the heart of it, this role is about relationships. It's about working across functions, bringing together teams from different corners of the business, and collaborating with third parties like advisers. It's about finding that balance between the serious work we do and the lightness we need to keep going.

It's the knowledge that, day in and day out, we make a difference – not for recognition, but because it's what the job demands. And that, I think, is the true essence of being a company secretary. The biggest impact, often the one no one sees, comes from working quietly in the background, with humour, grace, and an unwavering commitment to getting the job done.

LEADERSHIP LESSON

The impact of the work of a good governance professional is profound. It is felt in the calm they bring to complexity, the trust they build behind the scenes, and the integrity they uphold when no one is watching. The role has a unique perspective of the entire organisation and a high level of responsibility that requires quiet strength and unwavering ethics.

CHAPTER 4

CHAPTER 4

BREAKING THE MOULD

I work in the office two days a week, but somehow it always ends up being three or four. While no one explicitly requires this, the structure helps maintain momentum. What once felt like a constraint now makes sense in retrospect. However, encouraging new recruits into the office environment remains a challenge. Many are deeply attached to their remote setups, viewing them as essential rather than optional. Their reluctance reflects the broader shift in work culture. The world's changed.

Pre-Pandemic 5% of UK employees worked in a hybrid model; post Pandemic this increased to 28%.[32]

But I remember a time when that wasn't even an option. If the nursery called because one of my children needed picking up, I'd have to drop everything – papers, meetings, whatever – and race out of the office, leaving a trail of chaos in my wake. Back then, the office was *the* place to work, and flexibility? That was just a fantasy. Yet here we are, in this bizarre post-pandemic world, where hybrid work is not just real – it's the new normal.

If there's one silver lining to the madness, we all went through, it's that we discovered something crucial: there's more than one way to work. And more importantly, there's more than one way to live!

I grew up surrounded by law. It was in my blood. My family has its own law firm, a legacy stretching back through generations of uncles, aunts, and cousins, all practising together, like a well-oiled legal machine. The expectation? That I would join them and slot right into the family firm, continuing the tradition. But truth be told, I didn't want to. Not because I didn't respect it – because I did – but because I had this fire inside me.

I didn't want to live in a world where I was always 'so-and-so's daughter' or 'the niece of that lawyer'. I wanted to be me, to carve my own path, to feel what it was like to stand on my own two feet without the weight of the family name pressing down on me.

So, while everyone else was gearing up to see me in the firm, I had other plans. After finishing my law degree, I decided to throw a curveball and study for a master's degree. But not just anywhere. I wanted out of India, out of the mould that had been set for me since childhood.

I needed a fresh start, and for reasons that might seem baffling to some, I chose the UK. It wasn't the obvious choice. There was no grand strategy behind it, no deep analysis of career trajectories. It was bold, maybe even a little rebellious. But I'd made up my mind.

Around 75% of India's legal framework is based on British laws – there is an enduring legacy of British influence in Indian governance.[33]

Skipping the courtroom for the boardroom

Moving to the UK was about more than just education. It was about proving something to myself. To my family, who I love dearly, but who – like all families – had their own ideas about what my life should look like. I wasn't running away from them; I was running toward something: independence and freedom. The chance to be more than just another cog in the family machine.

When I first moved to the UK, I was 21 – armed with a law degree, a head full of dreams, and a heart full of ambition. But I also had one glaring problem: I needed a work permit to stay. That journey wasn't easy. My goal was to break into the legal world, but rejection after rejection piled up.

Every offer seemed to pigeonhole me into paralegal roles more junior than the level I was applying for; I couldn't stomach the idea of having spent six years in law school only to find myself stuck on the sidelines. So, I kept applying. One hundred and ten applications, in fact. And yes, I counted. Each rejection was a knock, but I refused to stay down. I can't say for certain whether companies fully recognised the value of my Indian heritage and background, but I choose to stay optimistic and believe that they did.

Approximately 52% of law graduates may never become practicing lawyers.[34]

But then, finally, one door creaked open. It wasn't a role in the courtroom – no thrilling legal drama, no high-stakes litigation. No, it was corporate governance. It sounded far removed from what I had envisioned for myself. But as the dust settled, I realised it was exactly what I needed. Maybe even better than what I could have imagined.

It wasn't easy. I went through seven interviews, written tests, and a long, tough vetting process. But something clicked. They saw potential, enough to take a chance on me. And so, there I was – sponsored, employed, and suddenly launched into a world that was a mix of corporate governance and legal work. That's when I knew I had done it – I had made it on my own terms.

My father had moved to Europe for work years before, but unlike him, I had no established career to fall back on. I was starting from scratch. And that rebel streak, the same one that pushed me to leave everything behind and forge my own path, came through in my work every single day.

It was that creative resilience that kept me going, because, without it, surviving in this industry would have been impossible.

LEADERSHIP LESSON

True leadership is born not just from ambition, but from the refusal to let rejection define your worth. When you carve your own path – fuelled by purpose, persistence, and a belief in your value – you don't just survive adversity, you lead through it.

A wave of discovery

Starting work in the UK was like being caught in a whirlwind. There were no defined work hours – it was just *all* hours. I was deep in a rigorous governance training programme, juggling exams while spending three hours a day on the road just to get to the office; remote working wasn't even on the radar. The grind was relentless – long days in the office, long commutes, long nights – not to mention the overwhelming cultural adjustment. I'm still not sure how I kept going.

But I did. Every day, I dragged myself out of bed, refusing to let the weight of it crush me. I had something to prove – not just to the company that had taken a chance on me, but to myself. I had walked into this new world with nothing but my ambition and my stubborn determination, and that's what kept me moving forward, even when it felt impossible.

In August 2024 the unemployment rate for ethnic minorities in the UK was 8%, compared to 4.1% for white individuals.[35]

Looking back now, I realise that the journey itself was the point. It wasn't about law firms or degrees or even rebellion – it was about having the boldness to leave behind everything familiar, to step out alone into the unknown, and to trust that I could figure it out along the way. That's something I'll carry with me always, no matter where life takes me.

An elephant never forgets

We've come a long way as a society. Twenty years ago, diversity and inclusion weren't the buzzwords they are now. Back then, people didn't really know. They didn't understand. And I felt it – especially during my time at university while doing my Master's.

I remember it clearly. People would come up to me, curious but utterly clueless, and ask questions that left me speechless. "Do you have a study at home?" one person asked, as if that was some exotic concept. The funniest one that really stuck with me – the one that still makes me shake my head, and probably always will, was: "Do you still ride elephants?"

In 2024, 13% of senior management teams in FTSE 100 companies were from ethnic minority backgrounds, and 13 chief executives identified as such (up from 12 in 2023).[36]

Amongst the FTSE 250 ethnic minorities accounted for 9% of senior management positions, below the 17% benchmark based on England and Wales demographics.[37]

I was floored. At first, I thought they were joking. But no. They were dead serious. And what could I do but smile awkwardly and shake my head? Now, looking back, I see the humour in it, the absurdity. But at the time, it was just tiring. The constant barrage of ignorance, the casual assumptions made about my life in India, as if we were all riding elephants to work and school.

It was as if they couldn't fathom that India was anything but some distant, underdeveloped place. Never mind the fact that I had to pay three times the tuition of a local student just to study in the UK. No, according to them, I'd probably gotten there on the back of an elephant!

And it wasn't just one person asking these questions. It happened repeatedly, at different places, with different people, until it became a pattern – one that forced me to confront just how deeply ingrained these misconceptions were.

But here's the thing – I get it now. I understand that, back then, the world was a different place. We weren't having the conversations we're having today about diversity and inclusion. The awareness wasn't there. Now, it's growing, and we're headed in the right direction. And those questions? They were just a reflection of that time, of a world still waking up to the idea that not everyone's experience was the same.

***Around 16% of FTSE 100 board members are from ethnic minority backgrounds and the majority of these are non-executive roles.*[38]**

From naivety to awareness

Were the comments racist or just ignorance? Probably a mix. I prefer to believe in the good in people, but after hearing the same questions again and again, you start to wonder. At first, I brushed it off – I was new to the country, and a bit naive. But I had already broken away from everything familiar, and there was no turning back. I told myself: I'll survive this. Whatever it takes.

My dad had encouraged me to study in India, where it would have been free. But I was determined to carve my own path, even if it meant facing challenges I hadn't expected. So, I let those comments slide, telling myself it was just part of the experience.

Looking back now, I see it as a learning moment. It made me more aware, and now, I'm careful not to ask those kinds of thoughtless questions of others. I try to remind people, and to teach my kids, that just because someone comes from a different country doesn't mean they're from a different world. We're all living the same existence – there's no parallel universe out there. Understanding that is key to talking with respect and empathy to people from different backgrounds.

LEADERSHIP LESSON

Some lessons come wrapped in discomfort, but they shape us into more thoughtful, inclusive leaders. True leadership means choosing empathy over assumption – and teaching others to see shared humanity where they once saw difference.

Cultural challenges

Being new I'd have to say the biggest challenge wasn't the workload – it was fitting into the office environment. Picture this: I walk into the room, eager to prove myself, but immediately I'm hit with culture shock. Take humour for instance. Everyone's cracking jokes, exchanging banter I can't quite grasp, and there I am, laughing along, not always getting it. The cultural differences hit harder than I expected, and I often felt a step behind, trying to figure out what was what.

Work, on the other hand, was a different story. I thrived on the technical aspects of the job. Each year, we had to present our work to a technical board – a panel of experts who would evaluate everything we had done. It wasn't just a formality; it was a serious review where we had to justify our decisions, demonstrate our technical knowledge, and prove that we were on the right track. It was no easy task.

The questions could be tough, and the pressure was real. But for me, that intensity felt like a complex puzzle laid out in front of me – something challenging, yes, but also incredibly rewarding. I thrived on that energy. It pushed me to think deeper, prepare harder, and stay sharp. It wasn't just about getting through it – it was about rising to the occasion and growing every time.

But the real test came during my secondments – temporary assignments with different companies. My longest was nearly two years at an insurance firm, and it felt like living between two worlds. On the one hand, there was the excitement of new work and new responsibilities. On the other, I was the outsider – not fully part of their world, and no longer fully part of my own. I existed in a kind of no-man's land: showing up, doing my work, but never quite belonging. It was a strange feeling – almost like being forgotten while still being there.

Yet, those secondments were invaluable. They taught me things I wouldn't have learned otherwise – how to navigate the complexities of the corporate world and understand the intricacies of governance models. But they also taught me about isolation. I had no family in the UK at the time, no real support system.

I learned the hard way that the office, with all its challenges and rewards, could sometimes be a very lonely place. More than anything else it was the challenge of finding empathy in that environment. The work was tough, but the real difficulty lay in navigating a space where you felt emotionally adrift. There wasn't a lot of room for vulnerability, and that, more than anything, was hard to bear.

How life has changed

I returned to work when my first child was just nine months old. It was brutal – no easing back in, no understanding that I had just gone through a life-changing experience.

It was straight back in, full throttle, like nothing had changed. But everything *had* changed, for me.

There wasn't the same awareness about the challenges of being a working mother back then. Juggling work with raising a child was incredibly tough, especially without family support. I'd rush to pick up my child, put them to bed, and then go right back to work, often late into the night. It was exhausting.

Thirteen years after childbirth, women earn 30% less per hour than men, which is driven not only by time out of the workforce but also by the limited wage progression for part-time workers.[39]

The real challenge came after my second child. My mum couldn't be there, and my husband and I were struggling to manage two kids on our own. I asked my employer if I could switch to part-time, or even just work from home one day a week. I was bluntly told no, and if I wasn't up for the full-time grind, I could look for another job. It felt like a slap in the face.

Looking back now, it seems unimaginable that this was just 11 years ago. The world has changed so much, especially with the rise of flexible working after the pandemic.

Back then, being a woman, a mother, and coming from overseas felt like an uphill battle at every turn.

Being comfortable with constant change

When I started in my first in-house role – working within a company rather than advising from the outside – I barely had time to find my feet before the news came: my boss was leaving. Just two weeks in, everything shifted. I could have panicked. Instead, I saw an opportunity. I wasn't celebrating their departure, but the chance to step up, take on more, and prove myself was right there – and I wasn't about to let it pass me by.

The transition from a professional services environment to a corporate setting, along with greater responsibility, felt like entering a whole new world. Everything was different – the pace was faster, the expectations higher and the way things operated was far less defined. It was a shock to the system, but I welcomed it.

The challenge forced me to dig deep into my resilience and grit, skills I'd been honing for years. It wasn't easy – there were plenty of long nights and moments of self-doubt – but I had the skills, and that gave me the confidence to push through.

LEADERSHIP LESSON

Leadership often begins in the moments when structure falls away and expectations rise. It's in those unexpected shifts that resilience, adaptability, and a willingness to step up reveal true potential.

High-stake deals

Working in a company rather than as part of an external advisory team gave me a whole new perspective – one that wasn't just technical, instead deeply commercial. I had always been focused on the technical side of things, but then I found myself in the thick of de-listings, massive debt strategies, and tax hedging across 40 different countries. One of the most intense projects involved managing the refinancing of £610 billion of debt; I had to coordinate everything and prepare all the legal and governance documents for execution to bring it to completion.

It was a colossal effort, but it taught me the importance of seeing beyond the technicalities – understanding the bigger picture of how these massive transactions fit into the overall corporate strategy. A major differentiator of those with deep experience of working in a company over advising one from afar.

Another defining chapter was a two-year, £80 million restructuring. It wasn't just a governance challenge – it was about sequencing the right people early, understanding the capital structure, and aligning legal, tax, and accounting at every stage. The complexity demanded precision across the board, from documentation to long-term business impact. That experience shaped how I approach every major project: strategically, proactively, and with an eye on both risk and opportunity.

LEADERSHIP LESSON

Learning governance from in-house roles is a must if you want to see beyond the rules and connect technical detail to strategic intent. Closeness to the organisation sharpens your ability to see the bigger picture, anticipate risks, and better protect the organisation's reputation within ethical boundaries.

Let me do the job first... then we'll talk about the job title

My next role was completely out of my comfort zone – my 'sink or swim' moment. I was thrown in the deep end working on complex transactions and integration projects that stretched my understanding of governance. We were acquiring nearly 70 companies across different jurisdictions. We were managing multibillion-pound debts, tax hedging, and intricate refinancing. It was like riding a wave, and every new deal felt like another sudden surge of intensity.

Though it was a daunting prospect, I couldn't resist. I thrived on the adrenaline of it all – there's something about a transaction with a clear beginning and end that just clicks with me. But I didn't change my title right away. I told my manager, "Let me do the job first. If I can handle it, then we'll talk about the title." For two years, I worked in the role, quietly proving to myself that I could do it before ever asking for the official recognition.

Working with 40 jurisdictions wasn't just about understanding laws – it was about mastering project management and building relationships. It taught me that technical skills are essential, but they aren't enough. It's the ability to bring people together, to create a network of support, that makes all the difference. The work will get done – someone will always do it. But if you can foster an environment where people don't let you fail, that's where you thrive.

I still remember my mentor, who wouldn't hesitate to point out things I'd missed, but never in a way that undermined me. Instead, the support afforded to me enabled me to succeed. That's what I learned: relationships and collaboration are the foundation of success.

You can't let ego get in the way – there's no room for it in this line of work. Pride, sure – but ego? It's irrelevant. What matters is creating a team that has your back, so you can deliver the best possible results, no matter the complexity of the challenge.

Employees with a mentor are promoted five times more often than those without one.

Additionally, 93% of employees with mentors report higher job satisfaction.[40]

LEADERSHIP LESSON

In high-stakes environments, it's not ego but quiet determination, strong networks, and a commitment to collaboration that elevate your influence and earns you lasting respect. Chasing a job title might sound impressive, but it's the substance of your contribution – not the label – that defines your real value.

Fighting for recognition in a legal world that doesn't always see you

I'm really proud of what I do, but let's be honest, it's not always glamorous. There are plenty of moments, every single day, where I think, "Does anyone even notice? Does anyone care?" It can feel like you're shouting into the void sometimes. I'd be lying if I said it didn't sting when people don't see the value of what I do. It's frustrating when your contributions are overlooked or taken for granted, especially when you know just how much you bring to the table.

That said, there are some who do get it. Like an executive I worked with, who still calls me the best person he's ever worked with. Those moments of recognition are gold, but they don't always come; I've learned not to expect validation.

But when it comes to lawyers, that's where my frustration really boils over. I didn't go down the lawyer route, even though I'm qualified, but that doesn't make me any less capable. What drives me mad is this assumption from some lawyers that their role is inherently superior, like we're the poor cousins of the legal world. It's this smug attitude that grates on me because it's not based on ignorance – it's a deliberate pretence. They know better, but they act like their job is somehow more important, more relevant, simply because it's been around longer.

This ongoing rivalry underscores the importance of the lawyer and Company Secretary developing a symbiotic relationship. Acknowledging this dynamic can provide a fresh perspective, emphasising that while these roles may differ, collaboration is essential for effective governance and mutual success.

That's when my ego comes into play – not in the work itself, but in standing my ground with people who should know better and providing education. Because at the end of the day, our work evolves, it shifts with the needs of the organisation; just because they don't see, it doesn't mean it's not there. That's the piece I'll always fight for.

LEADERSHIP LESSON

When others from different fields try to 'claim your space', it's tempting to react defensively – but lasting influence comes from calmly demonstrating the value only you can bring. It's on you to speak up – not to defend, but to clearly and confidently communicate the purpose and impact of your role.

PE firms

Let me tell you, working in a private equity-backed firm is like stepping onto a battlefield armed with a pen and a phone, everyone around you swinging swords of ego, pressure, and deadlines. When I first joined, the company had just been bought, and I was tossed into the aftermath of a delisting. The chaos was palpable; subsidiaries hanging in limbo, policies half-done, and new priorities that hit like a freight train. It wasn't glamorous – far from it. It was gritty, intense, and downright exhausting.

I started as maternity cover, temporary, just filling in. But within a few weeks, they made my role permanent. It didn't take long for them to realise, and for me to realise too, that this place needed someone unafraid to roll up their sleeves.

What began as managing subsidiaries and cleaning up loose ends quickly moved into something much bigger. Suddenly, I was neck-deep in corporate simplification, untangling governance challenges in tricky jurisdictions, and handling live trading entities while navigating the complexities of the delisting process. This wasn't just about shutting down operations on paper – this was real work, from streamlining customer contracts to managing insurance payouts. It was a relentless puzzle, and I loved every minute of it.

But there's this other side to being a governance professional that goes beyond just the technicalities. You're not just focused on legal minutiae; you're obsessed with the outcome. While the corporate lawyers are tied up in their contracts, we're zooming out, connecting dots across jurisdictions, regulations, and compliance.

We're the ones asking the practical questions no one else thinks to ask, like, "Do we have enough capital retained in that jurisdiction?" or "Are we compliant with customer contracts in this corporate simplification?" We're the glue that holds everything together, pulling in elements of our technical knowledge across legal, tax, treasury, and making sure nothing falls apart at the seams.

In governance, we're the problem-solvers. While others focus on assigning blame, we focus on keeping things running. We don't abandon our team when challenges arise – we push forward together, even when it's tough. Whether it's managing subsidiaries, overseeing policy reforms, or navigating complex restructurings, we make sure nothing is overlooked.

It's not just about solving problems, though. Communication is everything in this role. You've got maybe two seconds to get your point across to a high-profile audience, and there's no room for fluff. It's tough, and I'll admit, I'm not perfect. But I've learned that building relationships, investing the time to help people understand why you're being direct, and making sure they know you're on their side is the key to success. It's the process that matters as much as the outcome.

There were days in that private equity-backed firm where I felt like I was doing everything – picking up projects with no clear owner and running with them. I was also made secretary for the group's pension companies, which piled on even more responsibility. It was chaotic, sometimes overwhelming, but exhilarating.

The firm wasn't looking for someone to simply maintain the status quo – they needed someone who could help navigate the challenges of a rapidly changing landscape. I was more than ready to take the wheel, guiding us through every twist and turn with grit, determination, and just enough finesse to keep it all from falling apart.

High-flying documents

At one point, I had to organise a helicopter to deliver legal documents. It sounds excessive, but when you're working with high-level executives under pressure, normal rules don't apply. Moments like that taught me how to stay focused, adapt quickly, and deliver – no matter how unusual the ask.

There was this one executive, a true jetsetter, who had decided to retreat to some remote location in the USA for a holiday. Fair enough, people need their breaks, but we had urgent paperwork that needed his signature and getting it to him was proving a logistical nightmare.

Regular couriers simply couldn't reach him. There were no roads, no reliable delivery services – just miles of wilderness. And the only way to get anything out there? By helicopter.

It felt completely surreal – like something out of a movie. Here I am, just trying to get a signature, and suddenly I'm coordinating with a special courier service to organise aerial transport like we're on some top-secret mission!

To make matters worse, the executive had chosen such a remote location that communication was also a headache. I had no way of knowing when the documents would arrive or if they'd be signed and returned in time. All I could do was sit back and wait, hoping the helicopter would make it there and get back without a hitch. Most directors I've dealt with have been pretty down-to-earth and accessible when needed, but sometimes, we are expected to go to extraordinary lengths!

LEADERSHIP LESSON

Governance professionals thrive where others hesitate – in the grey spaces where law ends and judgement begins. Their strength lies in blending ethical clarity with commercial pragmatism, offering strategic advice that goes beyond compliance to support what is right and right for the organisation.

Hard times… You're on your own

In our role, it's not like we have a colleague sitting next to us in the same position to share a quick joke with. I remember doing a stint at a law firm where everyone was in an open-plan office, and people would come off a call, laugh about how difficult a client was, and it would create this light, relaxed atmosphere. But we can't exactly get off a call with the Chair and joke about them being an idiot for asking us to buy five stamps. We just smile and say, "Of course," like we're in some posh hotel where the staff steps aside for more "important" people.

Sometimes, being a company secretary is exactly that – playing the polite, deferential role, even when you're thinking, "Seriously, buy your own stamps."

It doesn't bother me much – I've accepted that's just how it is. But, if I'm being honest, I could stand to relax a bit more, let some of it roll off my back. Easier said than done, though!

> **LEADERSHIP LESSON**
> Governance professionals are expected to perform a polished, deferential role – holding in frustrations and maintaining diplomacy. Leaders must find a private "backstage" to decompress, so they can stay professional without losing their humanity.

Constantly managing up

Imagine this: we were in the middle of a huge deal. There were tax advisers, auditors, and a full legal team involved – basically, a high-stakes game with no room for error. And then, out of nowhere, the lawyers missed a crucial condition that should have been sorted before the transaction could proceed. It was almost a dealbreaker, and the stress was through the roof.

We scrambled, calling meetings on the fly, and I'll never forget how the time difference with the U.S. ended up saving the deal. It gave us just enough breathing room to fix everything. That situation was an eye-opener. It wasn't just about managing the legal and technical aspects of the issue; it was about managing people – upwards, sideways, everywhere. I had to corral the board, audit committees, and the auditors, all within hours.

That experience taught me a lot about sequencing – understanding how deals fit together and anticipating what needs to happen next. It's not just about getting the legalities right; it's about making sure the entire framework holds. And that's the magic of the governance professional.

The lawyers may walk away after the deal is done, but we're the ones left to make sure every follow-up is handled properly. Every milestone must be met, every condition must be managed, the integration must conclude without a hitch – you have to see the big picture, not just the finish line.

A frank exchange

On another occasion I walked into a board meeting, cool and confident, expecting to get a simple signature on a document. But the board of directors had questions – pointed, relentless questions. And I had nothing. I fumbled, tried to regain control, but the reality was clear – I was unprepared. Then, one of the directors stood up, looked me dead in the eye, and said, "Don't come to me again without the answers." He walked out, and I was left there, humiliated. That moment didn't just sting – it burned. It seared into my memory; a lesson carved in shame. I swore to never let it happen again. Now, if I don't have the answers, I'll damn well make sure the right people are in the room who do!

What people don't see is the sheer blood, sweat, and mental exhaustion that goes into these transactions and reports. They look at the polished final product, oblivious to the countless hours of meticulous work behind it – each word chosen with precision, each number backed by layers of evidence. And now, with regulators like the FRC[41] breathing down our necks, ready to pounce with demands for proof and validation at any moment, the stakes are even higher. You're constantly on edge, knowing that a single slip could lead to disaster.

64% of governance professionals reported high levels of stress related to board dynamics and regulatory pressures.[42]

It's brutal. It's relentless. And it's thankless. But here's the thing: I wouldn't trade it for anything. I'd rather be in this pressure cooker, taking punches and delivering results, than selling some meaningless product no one cares about. Because when I stand in front of the board of directors, through all the chaos, they know one thing for certain: they can count on me. And that's what keeps me going, no matter how hard it gets.

LEADERSHIP LESSON

In the boardroom, credibility hinges on preparation – never show up without answers or access to those who have them. Governance leadership is built on unseen effort, where precision and readiness matter far more than polish.

Building relationships with the board

My relationship with the board is a bit of a double-edged sword. On one hand, there's the formal side – meetings, reports, all business. Everyone sees that. But then there's this other side, the side that feels almost like a privilege to witness. I get to see the human side of them, the lighter moments, and even their insecurities.

It's funny – people often forget that these high-level executives are also being judged by their bosses, just like everyone else. I've sat in meetings where the CEO or CFO was getting an absolute dressing down by the board, and it's this unspoken rule that no one ever acknowledges it afterward. You just sit there thinking, "Wow, that was brutal," and then it's never mentioned again. It's like a secret code. You witness it, and then you lock it away.

These moments help contextualise everything – the strategy, the decision-making process. You realise these people aren't just their titles; they're individuals navigating their own pressures. Thankfully, in my current role, I work with a fantastic group of people – seasoned, sharp, and incredibly supportive. It makes everything easier, knowing that they're good at what they do.

What's interesting is how the relationship develops over time. In formal settings, everything is task-oriented. You're there to do a job, and that's clear. But it's in the informal moments – the chats over breakfast before a meeting, or the quiet conversations whilst travelling – where the real connections are made. These are the times when you start to know them as individuals, not just board members. That's where the trust is built. And trust, in this role, is everything.

For me, being in that room with them, being trusted to be there – it's huge. It's not a given; it's something you earn, and that trust goes both ways. The informal moments, the small talks about books or life, they shape your relationship in ways that the formalities never could. It's those softer skills, the ones you pick up just by observing, that help you understand how to navigate that relationship. And once you do, it becomes less about what's written and more about the subtle, human connections that hold it all together.

LEADERSHIP LESSON

Never underestimate the power of informal moments – they're where credibility becomes trust. For governance leaders, influence is earned not just through competence, but through genuine connection beyond the agenda.

From boardroom banter to beginner basics

It's a funny thing, really – this role puts you in so many different worlds at once. One moment you're sitting at a board dinner, everyone's relaxed, maybe a little wine in hand, casually chatting about weekend plans or how the kids are struggling to get into the right schools. And the next moment, you're in the back of a taxi with the CEO, talking business strategy right after an AGM, or catching a flight to a board meeting, trying to squeeze in a few last-minute details before the plane takes off.

Then, in the same breath, you're back at the office, sitting with a junior staff member in treasury who's never seen a set of subsidiary financial statements before, patiently walking them through the process like it's their first day on the job. Or you're fielding questions from the CEO's PA, who's scrambling to understand why there's yet another meeting in the calendar that no one seems prepared for. It's a constant shift in gears – one minute you're in "yes sir, no sir" mode with senior leadership, and the next, you're spoon-feeding the basics to someone who's still figuring things out.

That's what being a company secretary is really about – being adaptable, wearing a hundred different hats, and somehow keeping your cool through it all. And while I still take pride in navigating those waters, I must admit that these days, with more experience under my belt, my patience for hand-holding is starting to wear a bit thin. Age has a way of doing that to you, I suppose. But still, the thrill of it all keeps me going.

Leaders in governance roles tend to score highly on traits like conscientiousness, agreeableness, and emotional stability.[43]

LEADERSHIP LESSON

Don't underestimate the skill of seamless context switching – it's where adaptability becomes influence. Impact is shaped not just in big decisions, but in the grace with which you navigate every shift in gear.

Driven to deliver

In the end, it all comes down to one thing: I love doing a good job. I've built a reputation, one that drives me every day. My boss says that work escalates to the people who get things done. It's her reminder every time I feel like the load is too much, and it's true. That's my motivation – the reason I get up every morning and dive into the whirlwind of tasks that make up my day.

The truth is, I enjoy the chaos, the intensity, the pressure. I thrive on the variety, the constant shifting from one conversation to the next – one day talking to brokers, the next to corporate lawyers, and then meeting with board members and the CEO. It's that range, that dynamic interaction with people from every corner of the business, that keeps me engaged.

I've always been driven by the technical aspects of my work, and when there's no challenge, no problem to solve, I get bored quickly.

I need that spark, that something extra that keeps me thinking ahead, strategising, and navigating the complexities of the role. Whether it's managing budgets, handling stakeholders, or ensuring everything is aligned for the next big transaction, there's always something demanding my full attention. And I love that.

It's been a wild journey, filled with highs and lows, but I wouldn't trade it for anything. Every transaction, every lesson learned, has shaped who I am today.

LEADERSHIP LESSON

There is real power in the ability to thrive under pressure – it's in the chaos that we find clarity and purpose. In the governance space motivation doesn't always come from recognition, but from the quiet internally held pride of doing the job well, again and again.

CHAPTER 5

CHAPTER 5

A JOURNEY WITHOUT A MAP

I never saw myself in the corporate world. At university, the future was vague – I figured I'd try something, build some skills, and then move on. After graduation, I spent a year at a local firefighting company, just passing time.

Eventually, I landed at a multinational aerospace company as a trainee company secretary. It wasn't ambition that was driving me; I just kept going because that's what people did. I wasn't focused on climbing the ladder – what mattered to me was having a voice and being part of the conversation. In corporate life, if you show up and contribute, promotions tend to follow. Governance wasn't my passion, but it gave me a solid foundation, and that was enough.

Expanding my perspective with trustee exposure
Over time, I took on roles outside my day job, a trustee role in healthcare. It was my way of exploring what it might be like to act as a non-executive director, offering a different perspective and allowing me to apply the insights I'd gained from corporate life. I was surprised by how much I'd absorbed from years of meetings, and now, as chair of one of their companies, those instincts kicked in – knowing the right questions to ask and when to push for more information.

It's a different dynamic from my usual work, but the same foundational skills apply. Even when I ask obvious questions, I've learned that they serve a purpose – forcing the team to rethink their approach. This experience has deepened my appreciation for the role of non-executives, whose seemingly simple questions often highlight crucial considerations.

Interestingly, they specifically sought someone with a legal or governance background, which isn't typical (but should be). My broad experience has been an asset, although sometimes it can be a challenge when boards seek narrow expertise.

In the trustee role, we lacked the resources and corporate experience I'd seen elsewhere. Most trustees came from the NHS, local government, or education – great at caring for people, but not as familiar with running a business. It was sobering to realise that beyond caring for patients, we had to ensure the hospice itself was sustainable. My business skills, honed from my career as a company secretary, played a key role, giving me pride in applying what I'd learned to such meaningful work.

LEADERSHIP LESSON

Commercial and real world awareness sets apart the good from the great governance professionals. It helps to see the bigger picture, ask sharper questions, and offer insights that drive value – you become indispensable to have in the room.

Are the lawyers always right?

After qualifying as a solicitor, it took me a while to grasp how different the mindsets of lawyers and company secretaries are. Lawyers are cautious and thorough, often focusing on every possible risk, which can slow things down. They're not typically trained to think strategically or broadly in the way company secretaries are.

In the business world, there's a sharp contrast. Company secretaries are focused on efficiency and collaboration, always working toward the company's best interests, not individual gain. This broader perspective allows us to navigate emerging responsibilities, like Environment, Social and Governance (ESG), that others might overlook due to self-interest.

What's surprising is how ethical well-run businesses can be, often more so than the legal profession might suggest. Business leaders and company secretaries understand that long-term success requires ethical decisions, not short-term gains. For a skilled adviser, ethics and corporate strategy go hand-in-hand – something often overlooked.

Managing a dynamic with skill and poise

As the company secretary, I often find myself navigating the delicate relationship between the chair and the CEO. It's tricky, and there are times when their interests diverge, pulling me in different directions. I've learned that you can't always support both equally, and that's just the reality of the role.

When tensions arise, I'm often left bridging the gap between their contrasting views. It's not easy, but I've found that emotional intelligence is key. By focusing on what's best for the organisation rather than personalities, I can provide neutral, sound advice to both sides. The chair looks to me for big-picture insights, while the CEO expects loyalty and trust, which creates a unique balancing act.

A defining moment for me was when the chair and I agreed that the CEO needed to be replaced.

In most UK companies, the board can appoint or remove the CEO by majority vote, without shareholder approval, unless the articles of association state otherwise.[44]

It tested everything I'd learned – managing emotions, maintaining trust, and staying focused on the company's best interests. At the heart of it all, my role is about keeping the organisation's success front and centre, even when navigating these challenging dynamics. It's a constant balancing act, but by staying impartial and true to the company's goals, I can navigate even the toughest situations.

LEADERSHIP LESSON

When leadership tensions rise, the company secretary becomes the bridge – not by taking sides, but by anchoring decisions in what serves the organisation best. Emotional intelligence, neutrality, and strategic focus are essential to guiding through conflict while keeping trust intact on all sides.

Bringing those skills to the next generation

Reflecting on newcomers to the profession, it's clear that success is a blend of both nature and nurture. When you're starting out, much depends on the mentors and leaders you observe. Looking back, I realise how much of who I became in this role was shaped by the influences around me.

In the beginning, you absorb behaviours and values subconsciously, adopting those that align with success. Integrity and ethics are fundamental. The company secretarial role naturally attracts those with a strong moral compass, but it's not just about inherent values – it's also about the environment you're nurtured in.

If you work under ethical leaders who are both fair and effective, you're likely to follow their example and, without realising it, to start emulating behaviours that you see rewarded. But there are times when you'll encounter people who *don't* live up to those standards, and that's when your own integrity is tested. Do you go along with it, or do you hold firm to your values?

The biggest challenges I've faced, and what juniors will likely face, come down to choosing between what's easy and what's right. These are the moments that define you. It's crucial to learn from others, but also to trust your own ethical instincts. Ultimately, your career will be defined by the principles you uphold, especially when the stakes are high.

Knowing when to stay and when to walk away

Dealing with self-centred or less ethical senior figures is one of the toughest challenges in any organisation, and I've had to navigate these delicate dynamics carefully. You want to make a difference, but openly challenging someone, especially a senior figure, requires strategy. It's all about timing, influence, and knowing when to push and when to step back.

I remember working with a CEO whose decisions were more self-serving than beneficial for the company. The Chair and I agreed privately that we needed a new CEO as he was not the right person for the job, but we couldn't just act impulsively. The Chair had more leverage than me to implement the change of CEO as his relationships with the rest of the non-executive directors and the executive board members were deeper rooted. He progressed the conversations easily, but it was still a strategic process.

Throughout my career I've found that building alliances with people who share my values is key to gaining momentum for change, a good company secretary does not rely on open confrontation.

Sometimes, speaking up doesn't work – you get shut down or ignored. It's frustrating, especially when you know you're acting in the best interest of the company. Senior leaders who are self-focused can be hard to sway, and if you push too hard you risk being seen as disruptive and losing your influence – sometimes forever. I've learned to frame my concerns in ways that appeal to their priorities, even if their motivations differ from mine.

When dealing with resistance, you have to weigh your options: do you keep trying to influence them over time, recognise it's better to let go, or, if it's really bad, find another job? But in every case, maintaining your integrity is crucial.

You can't let someone else's lack of ethics drag you down. It's a long game that requires patience, diplomacy, and a focus on doing what's right for the company, even when you're working with challenging personalities. Sometimes you succeed, other times you walk away knowing you did all you could in the circumstances.

LEADERSHIP LESSON
People don't listen because you speak – they listen because they trust you. To earn that trust, lead with clarity, empathy, and credibility. Tailor your message to what matters to them, and when you speak, make it count. Influence isn't about volume – it's about resonance.

Finding justice in inherent injustice

In one role I inherited a highly paid team that was underperforming compared to their salaries, so I overhauled everything. In this same company I had to fight to earn the same salary as my less-qualified predecessors; this battle was about more than fairness – it was about survival. How could they justify paying me less for doing more and enhancing the capabilities of the team?

People often underestimate the complexity of the company secretary role, assuming it's just administrative. In reality, you're managing everything from governance to high-stakes projects like demergers and hostile takeovers. One of my toughest projects was demerging a business unit in the USA under tight deadlines, navigating legal and financial hurdles no one had ever handled before. A few years later, I found myself defending against a takeover – always knee-deep in technicalities.

I find the hardest part of the job isn't the technical work; it's managing the egos. At this level, it's all about balancing personalities. I've dealt with board members so consumed by their egos that it felt like managing a soap opera. When one chair threatened to resign over a simple company valuation report – it didn't give a rosy enough view of the company for his liking – it became my job to calm him down and keep things on track.

There's also the personal side of the job – like having to tell the chair it's time to retire when no one else will. That takes more than diplomacy; it's a delicate balance of compassion and firmness. One wrong move can blow up an entire situation.

People talk about "gravitas" like it's something that comes with age, but it's really earned through experience. It's built by surviving boardroom politics, managing difficult personalities, and learning from your mistakes. That's how you gain the confidence people refer to as gravitas. It's not some mystical trait – it's the reward for hard-fought battles.

The skills to progress

The role of a company secretary tends to attract individuals who prioritise collaboration and fairness over personal recognition. It's often about enabling others to perform at their best to benefit the organisation as a whole.

It reminds me of the first time you're given responsibility, like being a prefect at school. You have a choice: you can be the hard-nosed leader who rules with an iron fist, or you can be the one who's fair, the one people want to emulate.

That mindset sticks with you, and in a way, it's why so few company secretaries end up as CEOs or chairs. It's not about us – we're the ones willing to share credit, to stand back while others claim the spotlight. We'll avoid the chaos, but we'll quietly ensure the work gets done.

I once worked under a general counsel who was the complete opposite – a control freak who wanted to know and dictate everything. His need to be the decision-maker was exhausting to watch, let alone live with. He worked himself to the bone, sacrificed his personal life, and burned out. I realised then that I didn't want that for myself.

The company secretary role offers a more balanced approach – contributing in meaningful ways without being consumed by the need for control. It's about creating a sustainable path, both for the company and for yourself.

Jockeying for position

That's really the key difference between the legal world and the company secretarial role, isn't it? In law, everything is rigidly structured – rules, procedures, and this almost cutthroat competition to climb the ranks.

You've got law firms taking in hundreds of trainees, and it's a constant race to get to associate, then to junior partner, and eventually to equity partner. It's all about jockeying for position, and that competitive mindset runs deep. I think that's what sets the company secretarial role apart – we're not trying to outdo each other for the sake of personal advancement.

In the company secretarial world, we have to be creative, but not in an unethical way. It's about problem-solving within the framework, figuring out how to navigate real-world complexities when rigid legal procedures just don't account for the nuances of a situation. Like, you can't just hire a new chair for a major listed company on a whim right before the AGM if you've been tied up in a merger or defending the business.

While the law might suggest that companies should always have a chair in place, the reality is that hiring a new chair without adequate preparation could backfire. The process has to be methodical, balanced against the demands of the business, and carefully communicated to all stakeholders to avoid the appearance of chaos or poor governance. The rules say one thing, but reality demands flexibility. We have to find solutions that work for the business while still respecting the regulatory environment.

The thing is, governance is an ecosystem, and everything in that ecosystem is interconnected. Whether you're updating terms of reference, filing with Companies House, or crafting the governance framework, it's all part of the same machine. There's no ego in it – just collaboration. It's about making sure every piece is functioning correctly, because without that, the whole system fails. And that's what makes our role so different from the lawyer's mindset – it's more collaborative, more focused on the bigger picture, where everything has its place and everyone has a part to play.

LEADERSHIP LESSON

Governance offers a unique vantage point – when you understand how everything connects, you start to spot the pressure points. Like a tell in poker, the signs are there; great company secretaries read them early and act before the house of cards begins to fall.

ESG: where's it going?

Sadly, governance really does get overlooked in many organisations, especially when everyone's so focused on ESG. The E and S usually get all the attention – environmental impact and social responsibility are tangible, they're visible, and frankly, they're easier to sell to the public and to shareholders. But governance – the G in ESG – often feels like the forgotten sibling. It's less glamorous, less headline-worthy, but more crucial because it underpins everything else.

Focusing on governance isn't just about compliance or ticking boxes. It's about creating an infrastructure that allows the entire organisation to function smoothly, making sure the right processes are in place, so decisions are made efficiently and effectively.

As a job role we hate bureaucracy and we're often the ones pushing back against it. We see too many meetings, too many committees, and we know they can stifle decision-making rather than support it. The goal is to create a governance ecosystem that empowers people to act with authority, not one that forces them into constant consultation or endless loops of approval.

It can be counterintuitive to some people, especially those who assume governance is all about control – tightening the reins, adding layers of oversight. But that's not how we see it. Good governance is about streamlining. It's about trusting people to make decisions and creating a culture in which everyone understands their role and feels empowered to act within it. We don't want people dragging every little issue to a committee if they have the authority to make the call themselves. That's just inefficient and ultimately counterproductive.

And maybe, sure, some might think that's just me being lazy, wanting fewer meetings and less micromanagement. But I don't see it that way. It's about cutting through the noise and focusing on what actually moves the organisation forward. Simplification isn't a shortcut; it's a smarter way of doing things.

Governance, when done right, is about creating clarity and freeing people up to get on with their jobs, not bogging them down in endless red tape. If that's lazy, then fine, I'll happily take that label. But I think it's just smart, and ultimately better for everyone involved.

LEADERSHIP LESSON

Good governance isn't about red tape – it's about clarity and purpose.
The best leaders challenge unnecessary bureaucracy to make space for smarter, more effective decisions.

Look how far we've come

When I first started out, governance wasn't the sophisticated, multifaceted concept that it is today. It was more of a routine process, something that the company secretary did because it was necessary, not because it was valued.

I remember back then, everything was about the physical tasks – taking minutes, filing forms, keeping the statutory registers in these massive, leather-bound books. Governance was something that sat quietly in the background, a necessary evil for compliance, but not much more than that.

But things shifted fairly quickly. As time went on, I found myself getting involved in much more than just keeping records. Suddenly, I was handling intellectual property (IP) issues and mergers and acquisitions (M&A), doing real legal work even though I wasn't technically a lawyer. That part of the role was unexpected, and it required me to pivot, to grow in directions I hadn't originally planned for. Governance was still a part of the job, but it was evolving, and so was I.

The real shift came with the rise of corporate governance in the nineties.

Corporate governance gained prominence in the 1990s amid major scandals and concerns over accountability, transparency, and shareholder rights. The 1992 UK Cadbury Report was a landmark moment, setting principles on board roles, non-executive director independence, and internal controls that shaped global governance standards.[45]

When these changes started coming down the line – more regulation, stricter oversight – there was a lot of resistance. People pushed back hard. The idea of governance growing into this central, strategic function felt unnecessary and burdensome to many at the time. But, looking back, it's almost laughable that we ever saw it that way.

Governance has become such a vital part of how companies operate that you wouldn't think twice about it, now. What seemed back then like overreach or red tape is now just common sense – an essential part of running a business responsibly.

It's fascinating to see how, what once felt like a tedious obligation, has transformed into something so central to business strategy. Corporate governance is no longer just about following the rules; it's about shaping how companies think and act. It's about sustainability, accountability, and creating long-term value, and the fact that this is now self-evident speaks volumes about how far we've come.

Get used to being uncomfortable

One of my earliest and most uncomfortable tasks was telling the Company Secretary's PA that she had body odour – an awful responsibility that somehow fell to me. That incident, and others like it, taught me valuable lessons. I vowed never to dodge decisions or offload uncomfortable tasks onto others, as some leaders did.

I've also encountered leaders who believed my role was simply to follow orders. One famously told me, "Your job isn't to suggest, it's to do what I tell you." I vowed never to be that kind of leader.

I ultimately make the decisions and take responsibility for them, but I value the input and perspectives of my team. Leadership should never be autocratic, but collaborative – driven by a balance of responsibility and open feedback.

When I reflect on where I started, and the wide-ranging responsibilities I now handle, I realise how unpredictable this path has been. But every uncomfortable conversation, every unexpected challenge, has shaped my approach to leadership and governance, ensuring that I tackle things head-on, no matter how difficult.

LEADERSHIP LESSON

Growth doesn't happen in comfort. The best leaders embrace discomfort as a sign they're pushing boundaries, asking hard questions, and standing up when it matters most.

Ensuring that history remembers the context, not just the outcome

The way we approach writing minutes or papers should be to leave a legacy in ink. I always tell people, when you're drafting something, you have to think beyond just today. You have to imagine someone picking it up twenty or thirty years from now.

Will your words stand the test of time? Will it make sense to them? It's about writing in a way that is timeless – avoiding jargon, overly specific references, or assumptions. The context of today may not be obvious in the future.

Take the pandemic, for instance. During the pandemic, it dominated every board meeting. But I always wondered, what will people think in twenty years when they look back at those minutes? Will they remember how big of a deal it was? Or will it just be another crisis in a long list of crises? We had to be mindful of capturing not just the actions, but the weight of the moment, so that when someone looks back, they'll understand why we made the decisions we did.

That's part of what makes governance unique. We have to be both present and historical. We're documenting decisions in real-time, but we're also creating a record that will last for decades. It's almost like being a historian of the company, capturing not just the "what" but the "why" – the context, the reasoning behind each choice, and the environment in which those choices were made.

We appreciate the history of the company and understand why certain decisions were made in their time. It's not about judging the past through today's lens but recognising that what was acceptable or normal then might be unfathomable now.

I once worked for a company that had, in its distant past, insured slave ships. At the time, that was a legitimate business decision. Today, it's reprehensible, but it's a part of that company's history. When you document decisions, you have to consider how they will be viewed in the future. You have to ask yourself, "Can this be justified in the future? Will this stand up to scrutiny if it's on the front page of a newspaper years from now?"

It's a constant challenge – acknowledging the realities of the present while anticipating how the future will judge them. That's the art of governance. You're not just recording decisions; you're framing them in a way that tells the story of why they were made, for better or worse, ensuring that history remembers the context, not just the outcome.

Broad exposure gives us a unique perspective

I think what sets us apart is that we have a front-row seat to almost every part of the organisation. We're in more meetings than just about anyone else. We sit in on executive-level meetings, sure, but we also attend all the board committee meetings – places where most executives never set foot. So, we end up with this incredibly broad view of the company, spanning every layer from the operational to the strategic.

I remember when I was going through old minutes from the late seventies and early eighties. There was this fascinating conversation about limiting the number of computers in the company because there was a fear they would eliminate jobs. At the time, the trade unions were pushing hard against automation.

It's funny, isn't it? You see the same debates happening today with AI. Everyone's talking about how AI could either revolutionise the workplace or be a threat to jobs. It's the same underlying fear, just dressed in different technology.

And how many times have we heard it? Every generation seems to have its 'big shift' – the thing that's going to change everything forever. Sometimes it does, sometimes it doesn't. But that's part of what makes our role so interesting. We're intellectually curious, and we must be, because we're always thinking about how these changes – whether it's technology, regulation, or cultural shifts – will impact the organisation as a whole.

Our vantage point gives us a unique perspective. We're not just reacting to what's happening now; we're constantly trying to foresee how today's decisions will ripple out over the years. It's a kind of organisational foresight that makes us both participants and observers of the company's evolution, and that's what keeps the job so engaging.

LEADERSHIP LESSON

With a seat at many tables, governance professionals gain a rare, panoramic view of the organisation. This broad exposure fosters foresight – connecting past patterns to future risks – and equips them not just to respond to change, but to anticipate and shape it.

Another revolving door

Once, I was interviewed for a job by Bernie Ecclestone, the larger-than-life figure from Formula 1. Given his reputation, I expected something intense, but he was surprisingly charming. Later, I realised Bernie had a knack for distraction, like the time he stepped into a revolving door, spun around, and came right back out. His chauffeur witnessed it all, and Bernie casually said, "Tomorrow, no one will talk about what I said, only about me going through a revolving door like a lunatic." And, of course, he was right – classic Bernie, using absurdity to control the narrative.

I've also met other colourful figures, like a council member I once dismissed as an old relic, only to later learn he had been a revolutionary force in his time. It was a humbling reminder not to judge too quickly.

Then there was an Indian billionaire I visited for a meeting at his grand house. The towering front door was an obvious power move – making you feel small before negotiations even started. It was a lesson in how these powerful figures play psychological games. I always tell my team, "Don't take it personally; it's all theatre."

This job keeps you on your toes, whether it's eccentric billionaires, strategic revolving doors, or legends disguised as fossils. It's all part of the unpredictability that makes it so interesting.

Being unflappable

In this line of work, you learn to take people as they come. You stay calm, deal with what's in front of you, and keep your emotions in check. We're pretty good at reading people, knowing when to push and when to pull back – it's all about emotional intelligence.

At a drinks party in the USA, I was talking to a one of our directors who outside the boardroom was a household name. In walks this executive who barges right between us, literally turning his back on the director and interrupting the conversation without a second thought.

Now, you'd think someone like this director, with his career and stature, would be furious. But he wasn't fazed at all. It struck me how grounded and approachable he was, just like some of the baronesses I've met through work. I've found many of these big names surprisingly down-to-earth.

Of course, I've encountered bullies and egotists too, but for the most part, the people I've met – especially the intelligent ones – have been decent, approachable, and kind. It's the pleasant surprises, like shrugging off an intrusion with grace, that remind me that success doesn't always have to come with arrogance.

LEADERSHIP LESSON

Staying calm under pressure is a superpower. An unflappable leader brings stability in chaos, earning trust not by reacting, but by responding – with clarity, confidence, and composure.

Disgust

It was one of those situations that made me question my place in the organisation. A tip-off came about a senior executive manipulating expenses, which disgusted me. Before I could investigate, he moved quickly to attempt to terminate my employment with the organisation, covering his tracks.

The financial misconduct wasn't the only issue. The organisation was riddled with pay inequality, an institutional problem that had been festering for years. I couldn't accept this as normal – it went against everything I believed in, and the longer I stayed, the more suffocated I felt.

The breaking point came when the newly appointed chair asked me to reveal which board members had supported him in a private vote. The request was outrageous, and my answer was simple: "No." It was a moment that tested my values, but I couldn't betray the trust placed in me.

These experiences reminded me how crucial it is to work in an organisation whose culture aligns with your values. Some places, however, are different – the toxicity seeps into every corner. I knew I couldn't stay silent in this company, even if it cost me my job. In our role, we have the power to challenge what's wrong, to confront the CEO, the chair, or shareholders, and say, "This isn't right." That's our responsibility. It was one of the hardest times in my career, but it defined why I do this work and what I stand for.

Humour

There have been many highlights in this job, but it's the absurd moments that stand out the most. During a major takeover, we had a confidential call with about thirty people dialled in, but only three of us who knew the real facts of the situation. Halfway through, the general counsel started spilling the beans, realising mid-sentence that he was giving away sensitive information to people who shouldn't know. His voice just trailed off, and we all pretended it never happened.

Then there was the AGM when the CFO, after slashing costs, was furious that there were no chocolate éclairs left – his main takeaway from the meeting. Or the time the chair tapped me on the shoulder during another AGM to tell me there was no toilet paper in the toilets. One moment I'm handling strategy, the next I'm sorting out loo supplies.

I'll never forget when, after a long AGM day, we accidentally threw away all the marketing display boards and banners. It took checking security footage to realise we'd saved the rubbish instead of the marketing materials – but we managed to retrieve everything just in time.

And then there was the courier who took the CEO's papers by mistake, leading us to dash across London like it was some action movie. We couldn't let the CEO realise they were gone. And then there was the chair with his habit of firing catering managers if the lunch didn't meet his ridiculous standards, once asking me, "What's the provenance of this summer fishcake?" You could feel the terror in the room every time fish was served!

This job keeps you on your toes, from million-pound deals to toilet paper.

LEADERSHIP LESSON

In tough times, humour is a quiet form of resilience. It doesn't solve the problem, but it lightens the load – helping teams stay grounded, connected, and human when the pressure is at its highest.

Retaining your humanity

In the end, you have to laugh. Between the high-stakes drama and the absurd moments, it's a wild ride. But honestly, it's those bizarre, hilarious situations that make it all worth it. At its core, the role is about being fair – whether delivering tough news or navigating through quirky requests like explaining the origin of a fishcake to a chair.

Being a company secretary is about getting the right information to the right people at the right time so they can make informed decisions. And while you might be racing to recover lost papers or managing an unexpected toilet paper crisis, the heart of it all is clarity, fairness, and a sense of humour to keep things grounded. Not everyone will like every decision you make, but hopefully, they will understand the intent behind it.

What really makes it fulfilling, though, is the impact on people's careers – helping someone find their way, reigniting that spark in those who are struggling. That's what lasts. That's the part that sticks with me – the pride in seeing others thrive, knowing you've made a difference by being tough when needed, but always fair.

It's also about showing others that you don't have to compromise your values to succeed in this line of work. You can be decent, ethical, and still thrive. That's the message I hope I've passed on. That's the legacy I want to leave.

CHAPTER 6

CHAPTER 6

DEADLINES AND DOLLAR SIGNS

Today has been a whirlwind. It's our first year of being US-listed, which has meant dealing with the US-style financial statements, the 20F, on top of everything else. Oh, and we had to move our reporting date, which has compressed our timetable for delivery – so, yeah, it's been chaos. Managing multiple projects all within an impossible timeframe… you can imagine the stress. But somehow, we pulled together and made it work. The share plans, though – that's always the tricky bit.

It's this side project we handle in our 'spare time,' and the US listing only made it more complex. When it gets personal – especially when it affects their own share plans – you see senior people become very protective and involved, whereas if it doesn't impact them directly, they tend to be much more blasé. It's in those moments you really see a different side to people, and it reminds us to refocus our work and stay objective, even when emotions run high. But hey, we got through it.

From textiles to the boardroom
I never planned to end up here – like many others, I fell into it completely by accident. Fresh out of a graduate training program in merchandising, I thought I was on the path to becoming a fashion buyer. But that world was too competitive, so I settled for merchandising. Things seemed fine, until the business unit I worked for got swept up in the chaos of a corporate buyout.

Enter a famous British retail tycoon known for building a fashion empire, infamous for lavish spending, controversial business practices, and a high-profile scandal involving his brand's pension fund. He sold us off, only to come back and buy the company again. The whole ordeal left me at a crossroads.

One day, amidst the uncertainty, someone from human resources tapped me on the shoulder and asked, "Ever thought about being a company secretary?" I hadn't. But with redundancy looming and rent to pay, I figured, why not? I'd give it a shot, just for a couple of weeks, or so I thought.

Those first weeks were rough. The previous interim company secretary, who'd been given notice, was none too pleased about me stepping in. And she made it clear, pulling me aside to say, "I know you're not serious about this. You'd have started your exams by now." It stung, and to be honest, I wasn't even sure what the role really entailed. But I kept my head down, doing bits and pieces of whatever was thrown my way. And before I knew it, I was swept up into this new world.

62% of individuals struggle with imposter syndrome regularly or daily [...] especially in high-pressure or leadership roles.[46]

The funny thing is, I never truly felt like I had found *my thing*. I wasn't exceptional at any one thing, but I was pretty decent at a lot of things – numbers, writing, problem-solving, you name it. I could string a sentence together, grasp complex ideas, and just... get things done. And that, I think, is the story for many Company Secretaries. We're the ones who step up and say, "I don't know how to do this, but I'll figure it out."

When I changed roles, the new company offered to sponsor my chartered governance exams, but their overly strict reimbursement program had the opposite effect. The terms were so draconian that staying would have meant locking myself into a three-year commitment post-completion. Three years! It was too much of a sacrifice, so I left. (Employers beware: harsh conditions for training can drive away talent, even when the intention is to invest in them.)

It's also crucial to pay attention to the warning signs when choosing a company. I once joined an American oil company, thinking it was the right fit. But within hours, I realised I had made a big mistake.

The role wasn't what I expected, the way leaders spoke to each other was in my view disrespectful and the way managers 'managed' was like a dictatorship, in short, the culture was awful! I knew almost immediately that it wasn't right for me.

That experience taught me to do thorough research on a company before accepting an offer. Job descriptions, culture, and expectations need to align – otherwise, you'll find yourself looking for the exit before you've even unpacked.

LEADERSHIP LESSON

Culture fit matters in every role, but in governance, it's critical. When you're at the heart of an organisation – advising on ethics, decision-making, and accountability – you're not just working within the culture, you're helping to uphold and shape it. If your values don't align the tension will be constant.

Finding your own way… and nailing it

I had joined as assistant company secretary in a listed publishing company, and from day one, it was clear the company secretary didn't have a clue what she was doing. She was defensive, incapable of accepting guidance, and I quickly realised if I wanted to succeed, I'd have to figure everything out on my own!

One day, she handed me a monumental task: convert the company from a PLC back to a private entity. Her exact instructions? "Work it out for yourself." So, I did. I hit the books, learned everything I could. I even had to type up the company's articles of association (the legal rule book of the company) from scratch. Every step felt like fumbling in the dark.

After days of meticulous work, I submitted the final package. To my surprise, external counsel reviewed it and praised the thoroughness. For the first time, I realised that despite feeling lost, I had navigated through something complex – and succeeded. It was a lightbulb moment. Sometimes, when no one gives you feedback, it's because you've nailed it!

70% of learning and development happens through on-the-job experiences, 20% through interactions with others, and 10% through formal education.[47]

No news is good news

One of my past bosses once told me, "The CEO thinks we're doing a great job if he never hears from us." Back then, governance wasn't the hot topic it is today, but that statement set my expectations. I realised at that point that if everything's running smoothly, there's no need for praise – because there's no crisis to manage. *Quiet efficiency* became my mantra.

These days, my boss and I joke about it. He knows I don't handle praise well, so he'll quip, "That was very adequate. Well done." And I just laugh, knowing that doing my job right means staying under the radar. Sometimes, the best affirmation is no chaos at all.

The only one with a bird's-eye view...

There was this one time that still stays with me – one of those career-defining moments where everything was on the line. I had flown to the USA for what was supposed to be a routine discussion about ESG (environment, social and governance), but that conversation never happened. The moment I stepped out of the elevator, it hit me – a crisis had erupted, and all hell was breaking loose.

We had this one product, our main revenue driver, and the market was blindsided by a generic competitor we thought would never dare to take the risk. Our advisers had assured us it wouldn't happen, but it did. In an instant, the future of our company was hanging by a thread. Revenues could vanish overnight. Tensions were high – no one knew exactly how much trouble we were in. Whispers from suppliers were circulating, and we were trying to piece it all together. Meanwhile, outside the company, people were catching wind of the chaos.

But that wasn't even the worst of it. While the team was frantically battling this fire, I started picking up on whispers about a second problem. We had just launched what was supposed to be a blockbuster product – our big hope for the future – and it was crashing and burning in the market. The commercial team was failing, and no one seemed to notice amid the other crisis.

I remember taking the CFO aside and saying, "What's going on with this new product?" His face said it all. We had predicted revenue of $120 million, but people were saying we'd be lucky to scrape together $10 million. It was a catastrophe in the making – and yet, everyone was too distracted to see it.

Within twenty-four hours, we had to issue a profit warning. For those who don't know, this is a company's early alert to investors, signalling that its income will fall short of forecasts – it manages expectations and prepares the market for lower-than-anticipated financial results, but tends to result in a steep fall in the share price and higher scrutiny by regulators over everything the company does. I think back to that moment and wonder: if I hadn't connected the dots, what would have happened?

Everyone was so focused on the fire at hand that they were missing the bigger issue – the future of the company was slipping away. It felt terrifying, stepping into that chaos and raising the alarm, but I knew I must else the whole company would be heading for administration. The Board of Directors were the only ones who could authorise the release of the profit warning to the financial market. Additionally the executive directors and their executive leadership team would need as much time as possible if they stood a chance of successfully averting financial ruin.

The lesson I took from that: You have to know when to speak up, even if it feels like the ground is crumbling beneath you. It's not about raising the alarm every time something small goes wrong. But when the future's on the line, you have to be brave enough to say, "I think we've got a problem," no matter the risks. That's how careers are made – or broken.

One key aspect was my relationship with the CFO at the time – we had built a strong level of trust, allowing me to speak frankly. But beyond that, it was about piecing together the full picture. Sitting in the boardroom, you hear what management presents to the board, review the press releases, and see what the company communicates to investors. Then, you talk to people in the business – legal, commercial – and sometimes the narratives don't align.

You need to stay aware and really grasp what's happening across the business, and that's the toughest part. It took me years to fully understand how the business operates, what's truly important, and what drives investor sentiment. Reading broker notes, seeing what investors focus on, and reflecting that back to the team has been crucial. It's a unique vantage point that few in the organisation have.

LEADERSHIP LESSON

In business, it's not ignorance that causes the most damage – it's blind spots. Success depends on seeing the full picture, especially the parts no one's talking about. Governance professionals have the unique ability to connect the dots across the business, and when they speak up, they can change the course of the company.

Honing your spidey senses

Sometimes you feel that pull – that nagging feeling in your gut that something's off, and it's time to speak up. It's in those moments that you must be brave, but also strategic. Investors can be an invaluable ally. They're tuned in, often from an external perspective, and can help validate that feeling. They may not know what the board knows, but their instincts are sharp. Building that surround sound – your trusted network – is key.

But here's the tricky part: you have to pick your moments carefully. Be too vocal, too often, and people will start to tune you out. So, you save those moments, like pulling out a trump card, knowing that if you play it right, it can change the entire game.

I wasn't always able to do this. In earlier roles, I'd have hesitated, perhaps raised concerns quietly to my line manager. It takes time, experience, and a certain corporate culture to find the courage to speak up, especially in high-stakes situations. I've only had a few moments where I felt compelled to go straight to the non-executive chair – those moments are rare, but when they come, you know they're serious.

People are correct c.91% of the time when relying on intuition in business contexts.[48]

LEADERSHIP LESSON

Governance professionals, like psychologists, develop sharp intuition – not just for rules, but for people. Working closely with leaders, they learn to read tone, timing, and trust, knowing that in governance, what's sensed is often as important as what's said.

The power to implement change or resign

I once worked with a general counsel (GC) – an unusual character – who said something that's stayed with me. He believed every GC should have a financial cushion before stepping into the role. His reasoning? So that if a moment of principle arose, they'd have the freedom to walk away. It struck a chord with me.

What does it really take to stand so firmly by your values that you'd be prepared to resign? That thought has never quite left me. And I believe it applies just as much to a good company secretary. Integrity must come first. Sometimes, when change is refused, walking away is the most principled option on the table.

Being the "sensible person" in a business setting, particularly when facing visionary or creative minds, can feel like a challenging role. This is especially true when those individuals are more senior or have a louder voice in the room. However, both perspectives – creative and pragmatic – are crucial. It's about finding balance and recognising the importance of timing.

While the visionary drives innovation, the sensible voice, like that of the company secretary, ensures that these ideas are implemented within the boundaries of legality and compliance. The company secretary might occasionally feel like the "bad guy" for stopping a bold but risky idea, but this role adds immense value. Without this oversight, the company could easily veer into dangerous territory, risking not only compliance issues but also the long-term stability of the business.

What's key is trust. Senior leaders and creative teams need to trust that the company secretary's input isn't about stifling innovation but about protecting the business from unnecessary risk.

Sometimes, safeguarding the company from non-compliance or legal risk can be seen as "boring" compared to bold visionary strategies. Yet, the work of the company secretary lays the foundation that allows these creative ideas to flourish safely. In this way, it's less about being opposing forces and more about working in tandem – each playing a necessary role at the right time.

In short, the "sensible" input from the company secretary is about creating space for visionary ideas to thrive within safe, compliant frameworks.

Organisations with high psychological safety report a 34% increase in innovation outcomes and are 21 times more likely to benefit from proactive idea-sharing.[49]

Recently, we faced a challenge at the board level when the chair pointed out that our governance framework was bogged down with too much compliance. The committee structures were to blame, and they turned to me to fix it.

So, I took the reins and restructured the whole thing. I cut the number of committee meetings, which were too frequent; whilst a number of the members just enjoyed the intellectual debates, they didn't actually add any value. So, the unnecessary meetings went and new focused, high-quality, impactful conversations emerged... and they say governance creates bureaucracy! Only if you don't know what you're doing...

The key to making it all work, and getting others to buy into the changes, is in helping the chairs set clear agendas and expectations while redirecting the focus on what truly drives the strategic agenda forward.

Our next challenge was to introduce the same at the management level, where some committees are well-managed, but others exist simply for the sake of existing – without clear purpose or focus. It's a fine line between stepping in to help and accidentally managing everything ourselves, which isn't our role. But cutting through the noise and pushing the business to be sharper, more efficient – that's where we make a difference.

What a prison sentence taught me about crisis management
Crisis is something I have more experience with than I'd like to admit. One of the most defining moments of my career was the evening we were indicted. We had known it was coming – months of threats had made that clear – so we had a crisis readiness plan in place and brought in a brilliant crisis-management expert.

Strangely enough, despite the gravity of the situation, it turned into a positive experience, because everything was handled with such calm. The key was preparation. We had rehearsed for this and there was no running around with our hair on fire.

Companies that managed crises effectively experienced an average 5% increase in shareholder value post-crisis. In contrast, companies that handled crises poorly suffered a 15% decrease in shareholder value over the same period.[50]

What I learned is that crisis doesn't have to mean chaos; it's all about sharp communication and methodical action. The first step for me was getting on the phone to the brokers. We needed to issue a market release immediately – no question about it. But then came the harder part: how do we handle the internal messaging?
We had spent so much time reassuring our staff that everything was fine, that we hadn't done anything wrong – and yet here we were, having paid a substantial settlement, and with our founder facing jail time. The disconnect between our reassurances and the harsh reality was jarring, and we had to address it head-on.

Navigating through this required the right expertise. You can't do it all yourself. You pull in your resources: talk to the brokers, get the lawyers involved, engage the public relations and crisis-management consultants.

Every message needed to be delivered quickly and consistently, tailored to its specific audience but perfectly aligned across the board. Whether it was drafting the release for the market, preparing answers for senior leaders to deliver to their teams, or coordinating with external advisers, the response had to feel controlled and cohesive.

Of course, the emotional impact came later, especially when our former colleague – our founder – was sentenced and imprisoned. Even though his sentencing wasn't technically tied to the company anymore, it hit hard. This person had built the company from the ground up, and people were shocked.

Some viewed his imprisonment as a clear indication of criminality; others were conflicted, struggling to reconcile the person they knew with the situation at hand. And then there were those who saw it as a systemic issue, a failure of leadership. We had to speak to all of these perspectives, ensuring that our messages were clear, empathetic, and consistent.

As a Company Secretary, you often find yourself at the heart of this chaos. Whether it's managing the crisis itself or ensuring that all stakeholders are kept informed, you become the linchpin. Everyone else is focused on their piece of the puzzle, but you're responsible for keeping the bigger picture in view – triangulating messages, updating the board, and prompting the CEO when necessary.

It's about staying calm and collected, making sure nothing falls through the cracks, and guiding everyone through with a steady hand. Crisis management, in the end, is about staying grounded when everyone else is spinning.

LEADERSHIP LESSON

The best governance professionals earn trust across the organisation, building networks that quietly power resilience. In moments of pressure, it's these relationships – not just formal structures – that help boards access insight, act quickly, and lead with confidence.

Survival of the most prepared

When everything goes wrong, there's this moment that defines you. It's no longer about perfection, it's about survival. Once we accidentally published the draft version of our annual report on the main company website instead of the final signed-off version. An investor caught it and pointed it out.

Had that happened to me six or seven years ago, I'd have spiralled. Ten years ago, it would have felt like the end of the world. But now? Now, I've learned something invaluable: you can't undo what's already done.

In that moment, it wasn't about panicking – it was about action. I asked myself, "What needs to be done to fix this?" That's what years of battling through crises does to you – it makes you more tenacious, more focused. The shock and regret don't go away, but you learn to harness them. Mistakes happen, even if you've put every process in place to prevent them. No matter how careful you are, sometimes the unthinkable happens.

But what you realise is that dwelling on the "why" doesn't help. Sure, we'll dissect it later, analyse why no one caught the mistake, figure out how to strengthen the process. But in that moment, you just fix it. You gather yourself, steady your hands, and get the right report up. You deal with the fallout, manage the message, and move forward.

It's the hard truth of this job that something *will* go wrong. It's not scripted, and it's never the same crisis twice. The cycle of challenge and growth is what makes this role both tough and rewarding, and it's this that draws people in.

The constant change and unpredictability keep it dynamic. For any misstep made, you become stronger, and you realise that sometimes it's not just about preventing the fall but about seeing how quickly you can rise again.

69% of business leaders have experienced a corporate crisis in the past five years, and 95% anticipate facing one in the future.[51]

High-profile celebrities

High-profile people can make things interesting. One CEO I worked with was somewhat of a local celebrity, and I can say first hand that you've got to be careful with these larger-than-life characters! There was also a time when Jackie Chan casually showed up at a board lunch, as he was part of a celebrity collaboration with a famous fashion brand – because, you know, that's totally normal!

But, managing the egos? Now that's the real circus. One CEO ended up in a heated battle with the chair. Picture me, stuck awkwardly in the middle, trying to mediate this showdown like I was Switzerland. I tried to drop subtle hints to help the CEO out, like, "Hey, I noticed the board is asking a lot of questions about this issue." His response? "They should stop interfering." Yeah… no helping that one. It's funny, but also kind of tragic when a CEO just can't see they're on the decline. That's the real challenge – learning what presses people's buttons. And let me tell you, a lot of CEOs have some very, very sensitive buttons. You need a thick skin and a good sense of humour to deal with them.

Dealing with big egos tactfully

They've been there, they think they've seen it all, done it all, and know exactly how it should be. And that's where the challenge begins. You have to find a way to work with these personalities and still bring out the best in them. Take our current chair, for example – he's incredibly hands-off, maybe a bit too much so. It's a balancing act. I have to gently steer him, drip-feeding little suggestions, like, "Maybe we should cover this at the start of the meeting?" Then, when he forgets, I'm right next to him with a discreet nudge or a well-timed note.

It's all about understanding your stakeholders – what drives them, what sets them off, and when it's best to just let things slide. There was one CEO who was convinced he could win every battle, even when it was clear he was on a losing streak. But sometimes, you just have to do your job and watch things unfold as they will, knowing you can't fix everything.

The trick is reading the room, knowing when to inject a little humour into the driest of updates. "I know this is boring," I'll say, "but it's important, so just bear with me." It's a delicate dance – you can't overdo it, but sometimes, you just need to get through the tough bits with a smile.

LEADERSHIP LESSON

Emotional intelligence is one of the most undervalued tools in a governance professional's toolkit. The ability to manage complex personalities, adapt your style, and lead with subtle influence is what keeps the boardroom functioning smoothly – even when dynamics are difficult.

The keeper of secrets

There are moments in this job that leave you feeling hollow, moments that stay with you long after the day ends. One of the hardest came after making a profit warning; a deadly storm we couldn't control was brewing. We had to make sweeping layoffs, and I was right in the middle of it. I remember sitting in a board meeting in the USA, quietly hearing the changes that would gut the company.

What no one else knew was that one of those names on the list was someone who would be sitting right next to me on the flight back to the UK. On the journey home I felt empty. I couldn't say anything to my colleague. As we laughed at the airport delays, made small talk about our families, I felt physically sick. I knew that when I got home, I'd have to end their career.

It was crushing. You tell yourself it's for the company, that it's just business, but that doesn't help when you're staring into the eyes of someone who trusts you, completely unaware that their life is about to be turned upside down. I felt like I was betraying them, and the weight of that was unbearable. It's the kind of secret you wish you didn't have to carry, but you do – because that's part of the job.

Being the keeper of these secrets is a lonely existence. You walk around knowing that change is coming, that people you've built relationships with are going to lose everything, and you can't breathe a word of it.

You smile at them in the hallway, knowing they're days away from being let go, and you carry that burden in silence. There's no one to talk to, no outlet for the guilt that eats away at you. Maybe one or two people in the company are aware of the storm coming, and you exchange knowing glances, but that's it. You're on your own.

I've confided in the CEO before, but even that has its limits – he's still my boss, and there are lines that can't be crossed. And it's even worse when you don't agree with the decision. When it's not an executive with a golden parachute, but someone who's been through hell, who's fought through unimaginable personal struggles, only to be discarded like they're nothing.

It breaks you a little inside because you know it's wrong, but you still have to go through with it. You have to sit there, heart in your throat, and be the one to deliver the blow. And no one prepares you for how much that takes out of you. No one tells you how that sadness lingers, long after the meeting ends.

LEADERSHIP LESSON

Governance professionals are trusted with early warning signs, private concerns, and hidden risks that could shape the future of the organisation. They see the unfiltered truth, sharing in the board and CEO's worries and hopes. The key is learning to hold that responsibility with calm, discretion, and perspective – knowing what to carry, what to escalate, and when to simply listen.

A kick in the teeth

I've been on the receiving end myself, and it's brutal. The CEO decided to combine the general counsel (GC) and company secretary roles, and it was painfully clear that the GC had been pushing for it, advocating fiercely for their own survival.

There wasn't room for both of us, and the GC was determined to ensure that I was the one who had to go. It felt like being slowly edged out of something I'd given everything to. I was crushed, knowing it wasn't about what was best for the company – it was about self-preservation. I was a perceived threat to the GC. Instead of the company finding a way for both of us to succeed, I was cut loose.

48% of FTSE 100 companies *have a combined general counsel and company secretary role.*[52]

It took me years to reconcile with that, to stop replaying the moments in my head, wondering what I could have done differently, or if I could have fought harder. The reality was, it didn't matter – sometimes, you just don't stand a chance. It's a gut-wrenching feeling, watching everything you've worked for slip through your fingers, not because of your performance, but because someone else was willing to crush you to save themselves.

I remember sitting across from a seasoned GC at lunch, soon after I had left the company. He looked at me and said, "That must have been really difficult for you." I nodded, choking back the emotion that still lingered. He shrugged, with a kind of sad acceptance, and said, "But that's corporate life." It hit me hard.

Sometimes, no matter how good you are, no matter how hard you fight, someone sees you as a threat, and they'll make sure you're the one who falls. It's cold. It's unfair. But that's the reality. You move on because you have to. You remind yourself that, somewhere, someone will value you for the incredible work you do. But that betrayal – it stays with you.

I still remember vividly that day I was made redundant, and this overwhelming sense of doubt crept in. I found myself wondering, *Will I ever work again?* It's hard to describe the weight of that feeling – like the rug has been pulled out from under you, and you're left standing there, unsure if you'll ever find your footing again. I had worked so hard, poured so much of myself into the job, and suddenly, it was gone. The fear, the uncertainty – it was suffocating.

But then something remarkable happened. People reached out to me – people I never expected to hear from. Senior-level individuals, colleagues I'd only spoken to in passing, all offering words of support. It was humbling, almost surreal, to realise that these people actually cared enough to go out of their way for someone who no longer had anything to offer them professionally.

I'll never forget when a senior lawyer contacted me, inviting me to lunch. It wasn't just a polite gesture – it was genuine. Later, I learned he had spoken to one of our non-executives and put in a good word for me. It was an act of kindness that I never saw coming. This experience for me illustrated the importance of nurturing and maintaining a strong peer network.

They remind you that, despite the cutthroat nature of business, there's still room for compassion. And it's in those moments that you start to believe again, to hope. I remember that when I was interviewing for my next role, they asked for board references. I suggested someone I thought might be fair – someone I'd always had a good relationship with. When I received the reference, it was the most glowing endorsement I could have ever imagined. I sat there, reading it, feeling like maybe I mattered more than I had allowed myself to believe. That someone far more important than me had taken time out of their busy day to lift me up was a reminder that no matter how alone you feel in those moments of loss, people do see you. They do care.

Employees with emotionally intelligent managers are four times less likely to leave their jobs than those with managers who exhibit low emotional intelligence.[53]

We do it for others all the time in our networks, and yet we forget that sometimes, people will do it for us too. The kindness you put out there has a way of circling back to you when you least expect it. I've seen it time and time again – at post-exit events, where old teams reunite and look after each other, even after all the dust has settled.

There's a sense of community, especially in the governance profession, where we aren't competing against each other like in law firms or other high-stakes environments. We're just trying to get things done, together.

LEADERSHIP LESSON

A trusted peer network is a quiet superpower – offering perspective, support, and sanity when it matters most. Build it before you need it.

The joy of creating a little happiness

Many truly amazing moments in my career still bring a smile to my face, moments that just make me stop and say, "Wow, this is why I do what I do." We launched an all-employee share scheme, and because the share price was so low when the scheme launched it meant that when it matured three years later, some of the people working in our factory in Hull walked away with life-changing amounts of money, some as much as £150,000!

My team and I had seen it coming months before, and while we were waiting for it to mature, we knew there was a real risk that some less financially savvy employees might get caught up in the excitement, sell their shares, and get hit with a massive tax bill. So, my team and I put together a companywide communication campaign to educate everyone on the options available to them and the consequences of each.

We weren't asked to do it by management, we did it because it was the right thing to do. And the result? It was just beautiful. People – many of them on modest wages – were overjoyed, suddenly seeing their lives transformed in ways they never imagined possible.

That moment filled me with such pride. To see something so positive come out of your work, to know that in some way we had helped facilitate that – it was incredible. You could feel the excitement ripple through the entire company, and it was one of those moments where you think, "This is why we do our job."

And, of course, there's a lot of laughter along the way. I think it's so important to have fun in the office, to remind people that it's just work at the end of the day. You can't take it too seriously – otherwise, you lose sight of what really matters. You find joy even in the darkest moments, and it's those moments that keep you going. There's always something new, something unexpected, and that's what makes it all so interesting. Never a dull day, that's for sure!

LEADERSHIP LESSON

This role comes with quiet highs and private lows – moments you can't always share. Learn to celebrate the wins, however small, and stay steady through the setbacks; balance is what keeps you going.

Early experiences that shape you

Early in my career, I found myself doing all sorts of random, bizarre tasks. I remember sorting out street decorations for one company, dealing with individuals' parking permits, and even being the go-to person for getting tires changed on executives' cars. It was endless and, frankly, ridiculous. But that was just part of the job – if no one else knew where to shove a task, it ended up on my plate.

In hindsight, many of these tasks were clearly Executive Assistant (EA) responsibilities. While EAs play a critical role in supporting senior leadership, these operational or personal tasks are not the core of a governance or company secretarial role. Combining such duties with the responsibilities of a company secretary or governance professional not only undervalues the strategic and legal nature of the company secretary role but also spreads focus too thinly.

The roles of a company secretary and an EA should be split to allow each professional to operate effectively within their own remit. The company secretary should focus on ensuring compliance, advising the board, and handling governance, while the EA is better equipped to manage personal and administrative tasks for executives.

This division ensures that governance professionals can deliver true value where it matters, without diluting their contributions by handling tasks that fall outside their expertise. EAs are invaluable; conflating their role with the company secretary's can prevent both from reaching their full potential.

Fast forward to now: things are more defined, but that clarity didn't come easy. I remember during the US listing process going over the proxy statement, which is essentially a supercharged version of the externally published remuneration report, packed with legal disclosures. There was a meeting with the US lawyers, and it hit me – this was way out of the scope of my role. I found myself thinking, "Wait, do they expect me to manage all of this disclosure?" I had to laugh, but it was a wake-up call.

I finally realised I needed to be crystal clear about what was within my expertise and what wasn't. It wasn't about saying no to the work – it was about recognising when we needed to bring in the right experts instead of just dumping more on our already full plates.

Looking back, I wish I had pushed back more in those early days. The governance teams I used to work in took on so much unnecessary baggage just because there was nowhere else for it to land. But things have evolved, thankfully. We've gone from being minute-takers, hidden away in separate buildings, to playing a real, active role in the organisation. Now, we're part of the bigger picture, and that feels good.

But the challenge is learning to pick your battles. Sure, there are still moments where the role expands in unexpected ways – like the push to put the entire ESG agenda on company secretarial, which is absurd. We touch one part of it, sure, but managing the whole thing? Nonsense. What we can do, though, is bring people together, raise awareness, and make sure we're all aligned on the key priorities coming down the line.

Sometimes, it's about those quiet conversations behind the scenes, connecting the dots, making sure we're all moving in the right direction. That's where the real value comes in – knowing when to step up, when to delegate, and when to simply raise awareness to keep the ship steady.

LEADERSHIP LESSON
Governance is broad, complex, and deeply strategic – it touches everything from legal compliance to board dynamics, stakeholder trust, and long-term sustainability. To do it well, governance professionals need the space to think, connect, and lead – not just react.

Learning on the job

You can acquire the technical skills of a company secretary from courses and textbooks but doing the role well, beyond the first few years, involves learning a plethora of additional skills on the job in order to survive and thrive.

Someone I remember with fondness was a GC I used to work for – he was an experienced pro and I admired him for it; a terrible manager, but one of the sharpest men I've ever met. He taught me more than I could have ever expected. He had this uncanny way of managing relationships, and I learned just by watching him. When he pushed back, he didn't hold back – banging the table, making it clear where the line was drawn. But when he went quiet, that's when you knew something was brewing. Suddenly, he'd call a meeting, and you'd find yourself wondering, "Who's invited this time?" You'd leave that room realising you'd just been manoeuvred into a position you didn't even see coming. It was brilliance in action; masterful.

You pick up those skills from people like him. Sometimes, you have to say no, draw the line. But more often than not, you find that no matter how hard you push it away, the problem comes right back to your desk. That's the curse of the job working in a company as opposed to just advising one – you see the fallout before anyone else, and you know, deep down, if you don't step in, no one else will. And worse, if someone else does pick it up, it probably won't be done right.

That's both the skill and the burden of the company secretary profession. We're wired to spot the chaos on the horizon, to feel the weight of the thing that needs to be done, even if no one else can. You see the disaster waiting to happen because you can see the bigger picture and you're not part of the decision making so you can remain unburdened but for ensuring the decision making is high quality. This perspective is great but sometimes senior leaders and the board can find it hard to hear that someone else spotted something serious. And so, you do it yourself – because if you don't, who will?

LEADERSHIP LESSON

Watch closely, ask questions, and take mental notes. The people you work with – even the difficult ones – can be some of your greatest teachers if you're willing to learn from how they lead, decide, and respond.

Crucial relationships

It really depends on your business, but one thing's for sure: having a solid relationship with your GC is crucial. If that understanding isn't there, it makes everything infinitely harder. As a profession, that's one of our biggest challenges – feeling undermined in our role.

Building a strong bond with your financial controller is equally important. In reality, you end up spending more time working with the finance team than the legal team and helping them manage the workload is essential. That collaboration can really make a difference in how smoothly things run.

For me, another key relationship is with communications and investor relations. I speak regularly with our Head of Investor Relations, and he's one of the few people I can have really open, honest conversations with. They offer a different perspective, helping you triangulate information in ways that legal and finance might not. Often, they're an invaluable sounding board when you're stuck in the weeds.

And of course, there's the board. It's easy to overlook, but the company secretary is a much more pivotal role than people give it credit for. When things get rough, we're often the only ones who can help the board navigate through it. Having a strong relationship with the chair and key board members is vital. They're often the ones you turn to when the pressure is on, so trust and communication are non-negotiable.

Poor communication reduces trust in leadership for 45% of workers[54]

We all have bloopers

Sometimes I pause and think about the embarrassing moments in my career, as we all do. And while I might try to forget them, they tend to stick around for everyone else's amusement. Recently, I had one of those classic "I-can't-believe-I-missed-this" situations. A couple of our directors were reaching the end of their three-year terms, and somehow, in my mind, they just *hadn't* been around that long yet. I hadn't bothered to check the schedule, I didn't think I needed to. Suddenly, it hit me – a bolt of panic – and I realised I'd completely missed the renewal of their contracts. This was not a light bit of administration.

In our world we need to get approval from the shareholders for these reappointments once a year at the AGM... but the AGM had passed months back and they were out of contract. We couldn't just give them a new contract; we needed shareholder approval, and to call a general meeting (a shareholders meeting) we needed to get approval from the board first in a board meeting and then there was all the paperwork and meeting management set up so all shareholders could attend just to approve my humungous error. I had to own it.

My heart was in my mouth when I walked up to the chair: "I messed up. Totally missed this." I cringed internally the whole time, knowing that the date of the upcoming board meeting would also be the date of my very public humiliation in front of the board of directors. I could feel the heat rising in my cheeks as I apologised, expecting to be roasted.

The chair looked at me with a smirk and said, "Okay, but you do know I'm going to rib you about this at the board meeting, right?" And in that moment, I just surrendered. "You know what? Go for it," I said. At that point, what else can you do but laugh at yourself?

It softened the blow, but still – one of those moments where you want to crawl under the table for a bit... or maybe several weeks! It all went off without a hitch in the end, but that's still a lesson you learn very quickly – that whilst you might have the ear of the board and hear everything before even the non-board attending executives, your errors are also on show to the most senior people in the organisation.

Another incident came at the time of the infamous annual report sign-off – basically checking the final document for incorrect page number references, incorrect captions under photos and typos – seemingly easy, but after working on the document and reading it over and over again, for the previous four months it's not a piece of admin to take lightly.

We gather all the drafters of the annual report in a room for two days to scrutinise every single page of the report. It's like being trapped in a slow-motion proofreading marathon, but somehow, it's weirdly fun. There's an unspoken competition over who can find the most ridiculous typo – one year, someone discovered that autocorrect had changed 'subsidiaries' (a name given to the companies that sit in a corporate structure below the top company) to 'submarines'. Cue the jokes: "Imagine if that made it through! Have we secretly branched out into naval warfare?"

But honestly, those moments of humour are what make it bearable. You spend so much time with these people, staring at endless pages of dry text, that it's either laugh or cry. One of the running gags in our office, whenever the CFO says something a little, let's say, less than sharp, is for someone to chime in with, "Well, he's good with the numbers!" It's those little inside jokes that remind you how much trust there is within the group.

We can poke fun, tease each other, and still rely on one another when it really counts. And, let's be honest, sometimes the typos and little blunders are the most entertaining part of the job!

LEADERSHIP LESSON

Great leaders don't lose credibility by admitting mistakes – they earn it. Owning up, taking responsibility, and learning out loud sets the tone for accountability, builds trust, and gives others permission to do the same.

Finding my people

Over the years I've learned – and it wasn't easy to accept at first – that "good enough is good enough". It sounds simple, maybe even dismissive, but it's not. It's the wisdom that comes from realising that perfection isn't always the goal – sometimes it's about knowing when to move forward. We can get so caught up in the minutiae, obsessing over every little detail that no one will ever notice, that we lose sight of the bigger picture. And in doing that, we risk missing the truly important things.

Know when to let go, because sometimes the battle isn't worth it. That lesson has brought me a strange kind of peace, a realisation that we're all just trying to navigate this complicated, often unforgiving world. And in this profession, we can often feel a little put upon, sometimes overlooked, especially by those who don't fully understand what we do.

But we keep going. We share our experiences, connect with one another, and find strength in those connections. It helps, doesn't it? To know that you're not alone in this. That even in the hardest moments, someone else gets it. We just need to find our spaces – our people – and keep pushing forward, together.

LEADERSHIP LESSON

Perfection isn't the benchmark – progress is. In governance and in life, the real strength lies in knowing when to hold on, when to let go, and when to lean on others who understand the journey. You're not meant to carry it all alone – and you don't have to.

CHAPTER 7

CHAPTER 7

THE NEVER-ENDING JUGGLE

Life has been nothing short of chaos these past few weeks and today is no different. My husband was travelling for work. He came back, and I immediately had to leave with my board of directors for a few days. While I was away, we completed the purchase of our new house. Great timing, I know. Between that and the kids visiting family in Ireland, it's felt like a whirlwind. Now here we are – trying to move in, somehow juggling it all. We're taking a week off soon, and I'm hoping for a tiny breather... but who am I kidding?

My mum's been an absolute lifesaver, helping with the kids while I sort out a nursery. She looked at me the other day and said, "I don't know how you manage." Honestly, neither do I. You press on, because the road only goes one way?

Let's be real – the workplace still isn't all that family-friendly, especially considering most women need to return to work in some capacity after having kids. Sure, there's flexibility, but the reality is that work hours don't align with school schedules or the everyday chaos of family life. If we truly want more women thriving in the workforce and contributing to diversity, there must be some give. I'm lucky to have flexibility in managing my time, and the support of my mum, but that doesn't stop the mountain of work piling up. It's a juggle, and not an easy one.

63% of mothers felt that working flexibly hindered their career progression.[55]

The art of 'not for the minutes' moments

I think one of the most underrated tasks for a company secretary to juggle is that classic moment in board meetings where the Chair leans in with, "This is not for the minutes." I've heard this so much that I have to hold back a wry smile. Like, yes, I know. But of course, you have to sit there, pen in hand, frozen, because even though you weren't actually writing it down, now you can't pick up your pen without everyone thinking you were.

In reality, I was just catching up on action points from three items ago or reminding myself to ask a question later. But instead, you're stuck, mentally repeating your to-dos until the moment passes, waiting for the conversation to move on.

LEADERSHIP LESSON
Sometimes, the most important part of the role of a governance professional is reading the boardroom, not recording it.

Ditching crime and finding an unexpected new love

Ever since I was a kid, I was absolutely set on becoming a criminal lawyer. It was all I ever talked about – through school, college, the whole journey. I had this clear image in my head: standing in courtrooms, fighting for justice. But when I got to university and finally started studying law, I found something surprising – I hated criminal law.

The very thing I had dreamed of was my least favourite subject. Instead, I was drawn to corporate law, of all things. That, and family and healthcare law, though they felt too emotional for me to handle every day.

I graduated right in the middle of the recession, and with solicitor training contracts drying up, I felt a bit lost. Coming from a working-class background, there was no money for me to do the course needed to qualify as a solicitor, especially with no guarantee of a job afterward. So, I started looking for alternative careers where I could use my law degree and start earning right away.

My mum, who was working at an energy company at the time, mentioned the company secretary at her office. She managed to get me a week of work experience with her. Sometimes it is about who you know and leveraging your networks.

I had no idea what a company secretary even did back then, but that week opened my eyes. This woman was responsible for pensions, insurance, and a whole range of things I had never considered. She wasn't siloed into one area like most lawyers. I got to visit the Shard, meet with actuaries, and see the breadth of her role, and it hit me: there's a job where you get to touch everything – legal, financial, corporate governance, all in one. I was hooked.

After that week, I dove into research. I looked into everything I could, and within six weeks, I secured my first training position in London. And that's how my career started – quite the pivot from criminal law, but I wouldn't have it any other way.

From property deals to bruised bananas and starving cats

I've spent my entire career in FTSE-listed companies, and the journey has been a fun one! It began in a property company, right at the intersection of two companies merging. I was thrown in at the deep end, helping with a demerger and other major transactions. One of the highlights was being involved in the largest UK property deal (at the time): acquiring an iconic retail destination located in the North of England.

On top of that, we were simultaneously fending off a takeover bid from a US company. In just two and a half years, I helped manage seven shareholder meetings – in the usual course of business this would have only been three, but major decisions often require shareholder approval, and we had our fair share of those! I was part of a small but insanely busy team; I learned quickly.

After property, I switched to listed financial services. That's company secretary on hard mode! Everything is super-controlled and detailed; it's a tough environment. You work in such depth; it's almost a boot-camp for governance professionals.

Financial services require more stringent regulation than other sectors because failures in this industry can have profound and widespread consequences. The 2008 financial crisis serves as a stark example: it led to a 6.3% contraction in the UK's GDP and resulted in a £137 billion government bailout to stabilise the banking system.[56]

It's not for the fainthearted; only the strongest work in that sector for their whole career! I worked with investment banks, diving deep into the world of regulatory chaos and political chess games. At one point, I was heavily involved in a management buyout of an algorithmic trading business, setting everything up for it to spin out. It felt like governance on steroids; complex, transaction-heavy, and full of internal and external demands.

There were some funny AGM questions, too – all those typical ones you get asked as a company secretary: 'Can you locate the right-sized glass for the Chair?'; 'Can you find a cushion for the Chair?'; 'Is the Chair facing the right direction?'; 'Have you got the 'right' sandwiches for the AGM?' And then there are the complaints about seemingly unimportant matters, like bruised bananas, and even specific biscuit demands!

I once sat through a forty-minute one-on-one conversation at an AGM with a shareholder, in which my only lines were "Hello," "I understand," and "Goodbye." Sometimes you even get blamed by shareholders for things that aren't in your control.

Another time a shareholder attending one of our AGM's came over to tell me I was responsible for her being unable to feed her cats! It had taken her a long time to travel to the AGM venue and as a result she had not been around that morning to feed her beloved cats, somehow this was my fault and I was asked to factor this into the event time in future years!

But beyond the absurd moments, there are thrilling ones, like navigating management buyouts and structuring deals. It's always been a mix of serious corporate challenges and downright bizarre people-management requests. That contrast has made it even more memorable.

LEADERSHIP LESSON

True leadership means having the humility to listen – even when the feedback seems misinformed, emotional, or off-base. Being patient in those moments shows respect, builds trust, and often reveals insights you'd miss if you dismissed them too quickly.

Flashers and Feng Shui:
Behind the scenes of AGM chaos

My first AGM at a telecoms company was memorable – though not for the reasons you'd expect. We had a flasher shareholder in the audience, which meant scrambling to ensure security was nearby, just in case he decided to expose himself! It's funny because this one guy with exhibitionist tendencies seems to make his way around every AGM.

AGMs are so random! In a second you can go from talking with the CEO or Chair about important strategic issues to dealing with a lack of toilet roll in the bathrooms. There was also the time when we brought in a Feng Shui expert to bless the AGM venue.

As much as you'd think this would be a relaxing situation, just before the meeting started, the Feng Shui expert said they'd misplaced their phone, what then ensued was everyone frantically running around trying to locate it! With just ten minutes to go before showtime, we were pulling out ladders to look on top of the staging and around the set to find the phone while trying to keep everything on schedule.

Running an AGM is about managing everything from food to security. In the past I've also had to coordinate with the London Metropolitan Police, arrange sniffer dogs, and even ensure overnight security is on site to protect the venue. Then there's the detail work —preparing scripts for the Chair, managing tech setups for microphones and screens, and overseeing the Q&A sessions when shareholders ask probing questions of the board in real time. You'd be surprised by some of the questions we get.

They can range from the absurd ("Why are there three shades of grey used in the annual report?") to the downright bizarre ("Can I watch TV on my Nokia 3210 on the AGM WiFi?" and "why doesn't the company own Amazon Prime?") but that's the beauty of AGMs – serious business with a touch of the ridiculous.

Navigating the ever-changing landscape of corporate governance requires more than just a strong grasp of regulations; it demands an almost instinctive awareness of the shifting geopolitical and economic currents. ESG, for example, has become a dominant force, gradually eclipsing traditional areas like executive reward.

The new 2024 UK Corporate Governance Code includes the most significant changes to the Code since 2018, particularly around internal controls, reporting transparency, and director accountability.[57]

It's no longer enough to just know the rules – you have to understand the broader context, the political sensitivities, and the societal expectations that shape boardroom discussions. One wrong step, one outdated perspective, and you risk being sidelined in conversations that you should be leading.

But for all the high-level strategy, sometimes the job presents moments that are unexpectedly... human.

Take, for example, the AGM of a particular company I worked for. In an effort to make things a bit more enticing, someone had the bright idea to issue wine vouchers to attendees. The result? Absolute chaos. These vouchers became currency. Not in the corporate, abstract sense, but in the most literal way possible. People were trading them like they were high-value commodities. "Oh, I don't drink," one attendee would say, sliding a few vouchers to a fellow shareholder with a raised eyebrow, "but maybe you've got a spare tenner for me?"

I watched in disbelief as guests accumulated stacks of vouchers like seasoned poker players. At one point, I turned to one of our familiar shareholders and said, "Is that the fifteenth load of vouchers you've stuffed into your bag?" The shareholder laughed but didn't deny it.

Then came the food-related dramas. We learned the hard way that if you leave out a plate of biscuits at an event like this, they disappear in seconds into handbags, pockets, empty plastic containers. Everything gone before the tea and coffee even gets into full swing. The solution? Individually wrapped biscuits, allocated per person, like you would at preschool, one on each saucer as the server hands out hot drinks. It became a necessary, if slightly ridiculous, part of our event planning. I used to joke that if we left an entire spread of food unattended for even a moment, we'd return to find attendees stuffing sandwiches into their pockets like a survival exercise.

It's a strange juxtaposition – the weighty discussions on financial results, targets, governance, sustainability, and regulatory compliance one moment, and the utterly surreal battle over complimentary refreshments the next. But perhaps that's the essence of this job. Balancing the serious with the absurd, the high-level with the human, and the strategic with the strangely comical. And somehow, through it all, keeping everything running smoothly.

AGMs used to be grand affairs – hot buffets, wine, and a sea of shareholders. Now? A dry biscuit, a cup of tea, and a polite exit.

LEADERSHIP LESSON

AGMs are a key moment for directors to demonstrate accountability – not because of who's in the room, but because it's the right thing to do. Governance professionals ensure the board is prepared, the process is sound, and the company's integrity is on display, even if no one is watching.

AGMs:
Now with 100% less wine and 75% fewer shareholders

Post-pandemic, virtual meetings made us rethink everything. We tried moving our AGM to the morning, thinking we'd dodge the lunch dilemma. Smart, right? Except our HQ isn't near a train station, so anyone attending had to trek in or take a taxi. First year, we thought we'd be nice and put on transport. Not a single shareholder used the bus. Never again did we provide that level of service – such a waste of shareholder money.

Attendance is a whole other story. Back in the day we might get 750-800 shareholders. Now? Maybe twenty-five. And it turns out that if you hold an AGM outside of London, no one bothers to attend. Companies that rotate between London and elsewhere see it clear as day – attendance plummets outside of the capital.

And then there's hybrid meetings – an experiment in patience. I once had a shareholder call head office, struggling to get a copy of the Notice of Meeting document from our website. "Go to the website," I said. "What's the internet?" he replied. I posted him a hard copy and bowed out. He probably played me, but honestly? Well done him.

The other challenge is that hybrid meetings are a ton of effort for barely any shareholder engagement, which is such a shame. Sure, some companies are going hybrid, but we've kept it simple: live webcast, no live Q&A. Instead, shareholders submit questions in advance, and we address them during the meeting. It aligns neatly with proxy voting deadlines, and honestly? No one's making a fuss.

The in-person crowd is predictable – dedicated regulars who turn up no matter what. But gone are the days of freebies, meals, and making a day of it. Turns out, a basic AGM without the free lunch and a glass of wine doesn't have the same pull. Funny, that.

As of November 2024, 66% of FTSE 350 companies held entirely physical AGMs with no electronic participation.[58]

The boardroom:
Egos, sharp minds, and the ones who get it right

I've been lucky with my boards – no inflated egos, no superiority complex, just real people who engage, listen, and respect the role of a company secretary. Sure, I sometimes see a different side when they're dealing with management, but they get why I'm there, and the value I bring.

I feel that over the course of my career I've seen a growing appreciation for what a company secretary actually does amongst Non-Executive Directors (NEDs) – and how to use us effectively, too. I'm seeing more new board members understand governance and their own responsibilities, which is a welcome shift. The best NEDs are sharp; they challenge management when needed, support when appropriate, and ask the right questions. As a company secretary, you get a unique vantage point – slightly removed but able to see who's truly excelling in their role. And when they get it right, it's impressive.

Investment bankers, though? I've come across these during transactions and they're a different breed entirely. Not fun. Conversations with them are exactly what you might expect – transactional, dry, and often frustrating. Tempers can also get frayed more easily and you get shouty conversations, but these are often expected. The pressure ramps up, and suddenly, everyone's barking orders, demanding answers, and acting like the world might end if their call isn't returned in five seconds.

Workplace incivility is highly contagious; even witnessing rude behaviour can lead to a 44% reduction in team performance in high-stakes environments.[59]

Whilst middle management sometimes don't mix so well with the board, they work well with the company secretariat team; they are curious, engaged, and eager to learn. Versatility is a necessary trait of a good company secretary. The sheer breadth of topics covered in one day can be immense; advising the board one minute to being a peer to executives writing their board papers for an upcoming meeting and then supporting middle management in finance on getting the day-to-day transfer of assets or payments of dividends 'over the line'.

When shareholders show up: The unexpected side of the job

If you'd asked me my biggest challenge in this role, I wouldn't name the board, the executives, or even the most demanding investment bankers. No, the real test? The shareholders.

One incident whilst I was working in financial services still sticks with me today. It wasn't even a shareholder, but a customer – desperate, furious, and heartbroken. Their home had been repossessed. Instead of calling or writing, they showed up at our head office, children in tow, demanding to see the CEO, the Chair – anyone who would listen.

The situation was tense. They were distraught, their emotions raw, and, to make matters worse, the customer reeked of alcohol. It wasn't just a customer complaint; it was a crisis unfolding in our lobby in front of everyone who happened to be in reception that day.

Security had to intervene, but it was the company secretarial team that took the lead. We already knew their story – they had been attending AGMs, writing letters, pleading for intervention. The shareholder relations lead within our team, well-versed in these delicate situations, stepped in to de-escalate.

There are so many elements to the company secretary role that involve being empathetic whilst seeking to maintain the reputation of the company and secretariat department amongst colleagues and the outside world.

Organisations with high-empathy leadership saw 56% higher revenue growth compared to those with low-empathy leadership.[60]

And then there were the others – the ones who received a letter from us and decided the best response was to turn up at HQ, unannounced, demanding face time. No appointment, no warning, just an expectation that someone, anyone (but ideally the CEO or Chair), would drop everything to listen.

I get it, sometimes people want answers. They want to be heard. But there are moments when you sit there, reading an email or fielding a call, and think, *how did we get here?*

Every company I've joined has struggled in some way. Some don't even exist anymore. When I joined financial services, it was just after the financial crisis – arguably the worst possible time to be there. Great for experience, terrible for everything else. Even now, the company I'm at isn't exactly thriving. It's become a pattern. I arrive, and things start going south. Still, in order to deal with it I have honed skills that I just wouldn't have if I hadn't been through it.

For me, one of the key skills I've learnt is damage control. I've seen dividend cuts which have led to deep shareholder frustration and difficult conversations – those have been my reality. That's the thing about being a company secretary. You don't just witness the highs and lows. You're right in the middle of them, navigating without a compass.

LEADERSHIP LESSON

The toughest moments aren't in the boardroom – they're when emotion, risk, and reputation hit all at once. Governance professionals don't just manage process; they steady the ship. The lesson? Stay calm, stay human, and know that how you show up in those moments defines your impact.

A journey of growth, impact, and leadership

Looking back on my career, I can pinpoint several defining moments – experiences that not only shaped me but also had tangible financial impacts on the businesses I worked for.

One of the most significant milestones was my involvement in a major management buyout within financial services. It was an intense, high-stakes transaction, the kind that demands precision, strategy, and resilience. I found myself as the sole company-secretarial support on the deal, playing a critical role in structuring and overseeing its operation.

The complexity of the transaction was staggering – it was cross-jurisdictional, involving teams from different countries and legal frameworks. I had to coordinate across these borders, managing the legal and restructuring aspects while working closely with external advisers in various locations. Despite the challenges, the deal was executed successfully, and the company continues to thrive under the structure we established.

What made this achievement so pivotal for me was the level of ownership I was given. I was only about four years into my career at the time, yet I was engaging directly with senior stakeholders, driving key decisions, and proving my ability to handle high-level transactions. It was a moment that truly set me on my path, reinforcing my confidence and solidifying my passion for complex financial deals.

Beyond the numbers, another source of pride has been my impact on people. I've experienced significant staff turnover; I watched many of my former team members move on to bigger and better opportunities. It's a testament, I hope, to the experience and guidance I was able to offer them.

One of the most meaningful compliments I've ever received came from someone who joined my team about eighteen months ago. She told me that one of the main reasons she applied for the role was because she wanted to work with me. It was a moment of pure validation – not because I seek recognition, but because it reminded me of the kind of leader I strive to be.

I've worked under micromanagers and under inspiring leaders, and I've taken lessons from both. I aim to be approachable, direct, and down-to-earth. Hierarchies have never meant much to me; I believe in collaboration, in treating people as equals, and in fostering an environment where my team can grow. To have someone recognise that and seek out an opportunity to work alongside me was an incredible honour.

On a more personal level, the past few years have been a whirlwind. I've had two children in two years and, remarkably, been promoted twice – each time under a different boss. It's been a challenging but rewarding journey, one that has reinforced my ability to balance ambition, leadership, and personal responsibilities.

Each of these moments, from high-profile transactions to personal milestones, has contributed to the career I'm building. And while there's always room for improvement, I'm proud of where I've been – and excited for where I'm going next.

60% of employees report having a healthy work-life balance, with 67% noting improvements after transitioning to remote work.[61]

The weight of knowing

There's a strange, almost eerie power in being privy to conversations that most people will never hear. Sitting at the crossroads of leadership and execution, I get an unfiltered view into the boardroom – what's being planned, what's being whispered about behind closed doors. It's a privilege, sure, but also a burden.

Because once you've seen how the machine really works, it's impossible to be impartial.

I'll sit in a meeting, listen to ideas being thrown around, and in the back of my mind, I already know the truth. I've seen the board's playbook. I know which strategies are dead on arrival, which initiatives are nothing more than smoke and mirrors. But I can't say a word. That's the deal. You don't get to be in the room and then break the rules.

And it goes deeper.

Executive changes, restructuring – sometimes I know people are leaving before they do. I've seen the emails, heard the murmurs, watched the chess pieces move long before the checkmate. That's the unspoken reality of these roles: discretion isn't just expected – it's survival.

People think the appeal of these positions is the access, the inside track. They assume it's all about getting ahead, knowing the strategy before it's public, seeing the numbers before the market does, anticipating bonuses before they're announced. And sure, that's part of it. But the other side? The side no one talks about. It's seeing the cracks before anyone else does.

60% of executives report high levels of stress, primarily due to the constant demand to anticipate and mitigate potential problems before they arise.[62]

When things are going south, you feel it in your bones. You read between the lines of every financial report, every leadership shake-up, every coded email from the top. You know when a company is quietly preparing for impact – long before the headlines hit. It makes you hyper-aware, maybe even a little paranoid. Job security becomes this fragile thing, because you know exactly how close the fire is getting.

Some sectors, like financial services, are built to weather storms. Too big to fail, as they say. But others? The fall is inevitable. I worked with someone who was in the room when a company made the call to shut down. People were crying, knowing they were about to pull the rug from under thousands of employees, watching something historic collapse in real time.

I haven't had to experience that firsthand. Not yet. But I've seen enough to know that when it happens, you don't get to run. You're one of the last people on the ship, knowing it's sinking, unable to scream it from the deck. You just watch. You hold the weight of knowing.

And when people come to you, excited about the future, about plans they don't know are already crumbling, you can't lie. But you also can't tell the truth. So, you do the only thing you can. You nod. You smile. And you carry on.

LEADERSHIP LESSON

The higher you rise, the heavier the pressure – seeing what others can't, carrying what others won't. Real strength is knowing when to speak up, who to lean on, and creating space to reset. A trusted peer network makes the weight easier to carry – and reminds you that you're not alone at the top.

The balancing act of power and influence

In this role, you don't just take minutes and draft agendas – you become the confidant, the coach, the quiet counsellor for the board of directors, executives and many others. When you build strong relationships with the board, you inevitably end up being the person people come to when they need to vent, strategise, or – more often than not – navigate the politics of power.

And sometimes, that means handling *really* awkward conversations. One of the most challenging situations I've faced were NEDs quietly expressing concerns about other NEDs. Not in a scandalous, career-ending way, but in that *this-isn't-working-and-something-has-to-give* kind of way. They'd pull me aside, looking for a solution, as if I held the secret key to making personalities and politics align. And, of course, the next step would always be feeding these concerns back to the chair – delicately, factually, without tipping the balance too far in one direction.

Then, there's the *real* tightrope walk, major shareholders sitting on the board. I once had a NED who represented a huge private equity investor – the kind of presence that instantly shifts the power dynamics. From day one, he was seen as the proverbial fox in the henhouse. He knew it, too. Instead of voicing his concerns in meetings, he'd come to me, asking for changes in how papers were structured, how discussions were framed – nudging, but never outright asking for special treatment. I had to shut it down.

"These are board matters," I'd say. "If you want a change, raise it in the meeting."

Because here's the thing: as a company secretary, you're not there to serve management, or investors, or any one faction. You're there to uphold governance. And that means sometimes, you have to say *no* – even to the most powerful people in the room.

Which brings me to the moment when I was asked to arrange a board meeting *without* inviting a key shareholder's representative. "Just...

leave them off the invite. Don't tell them. Pretend it's not happening," I was told in no uncertain terms.

I had to take a breath before confirming that "unless we're officially declaring a conflict of interest which would legally bar them from attending the meeting, that's not happening."

It's these moments that define the job. You're in the room with the CEO, the chair, the board, and you have to stand your ground without burning bridges. The trick? Take emotion out of it. Be factual. Be unwavering. Offer alternatives when you can, but don't sugarcoat a hard *no*. And, in my case, knowing I had my boss backing me up made all the difference.

LEADERSHIP LESSON

When power tries to bend process, it's the governance professional who must hold the line. Their duty isn't to please the loudest voice or the biggest investor – it's to protect the integrity of the board. Sometimes that means saying no to the very people others are too afraid to challenge. That's not defiance – that's governance.

The dual faces of leadership:
Boardroom strategy vs. public persona

What's fascinating for me in my role is seeing how leadership plays out at different levels. You watch the CEO in the boardroom – measured, strategic, restrained. Then you see them addressing employees, suddenly more animated, more passionate. It's not an act – it's just the reality of navigating different audiences. In the boardroom, they have to deliver a cold, unembellished truth. But when they stand in front of employees, they're allowed to inspire, to rally, to show belief in the future.

Not every CEO can strike that balance. Some are all ego, all self-preservation. But the ones who lead with authenticity? The ones who strip away the pretence and genuinely want to do the right thing. You see their impact from the top down and feel it in the company culture.

A supportive organisational culture significantly enhances the effectiveness of a company's strategy execution efforts.[63]

LEADERSHIP LESSON
Culture eats strategy for breakfast – and it's the governance professional who helps make sure the culture supports the strategy. By embedding values into decisions and holding leaders accountable, they turn good intentions into lasting impact.

The bridge between the boardroom and the business

In a world where corporate hierarchies create invisible walls, sometimes my role feels less like a governance function and more like a translator – connecting those in the boardroom to the people on the ground.

There's a misconception that senior leadership operates in a bubble, indifferent to the struggles of employees. I've heard it before, whispered at the proverbial water cooler: *"The CEO doesn't care about us." "The board has no idea what we're dealing with."* And while I can't always dispel every doubt, I do have the unique privilege of being able to say, "Actually, they do."

Because I've been in those meetings. I've seen leadership grapple with real issues – diversity and inclusion, employee wellbeing, workplace culture. I can't disclose everything, but I can share enough to let people know that their concerns aren't just numbers on a spreadsheet; they're actual conversations happening at the top.

LEADERSHIP LESSON
Governance professionals play a crucial role in turning conversations about diversity, wellbeing, and culture into accountable action. By ensuring these issues are on the agenda, challenging gaps between values and behaviour, and supporting transparent decision-making, they help leadership move from intention to impact.

It's a delicate balance. I'm not a spokesperson. I'm not a cheerleader. But I am in a position to bridge the gap between perception and reality. When employees assume that the board is 'out of touch', I can offer insight. When leadership makes decisions that don't land well, I can relay feedback that might otherwise get lost in the corporate void.

The bigger the company, the more complicated the web becomes. Internal communications teams, HR functions, investor relations – all have their roles to play. But governance? That's the thread that weaves it all together.

And sometimes, that means sitting in the middle, watching as different departments chase answers they don't yet have, knowing full well that I can't give them the missing piece just yet. That's the unseen skill of a great company secretary – knowing when to speak, when to stay silent, when to nudge a conversation in the right direction without ever making it about you.

Because at the end of the day, we're not just keeping records. We're shaping narratives. We're managing power dynamics. We're making sure that the people in the room – the ones who make the decisions – see the full picture.

Even if they don't always want to.

The core skills of a great company secretary

If I had to name the top skills that define a great company secretary, two immediately come to mind: discretion and time management.

Discretion, because the higher you climb, the more you know – and the less you can say. You become the keeper of corporate truths, navigating boardroom tensions, sensitive shareholder concerns, and internal politics without ever letting a flicker of information slip. Knowing what to say, when to say it, and – more importantly – when to say nothing at all is an art form.

Time management, because the sheer volume of work is relentless. One moment, you're knee-deep in governance, the next, you're fielding shareholder enquiries or drafting minutes for a board meeting while juggling six other priorities. The ability to triage, prioritise, and still produce high-quality work under pressure is what keeps everything from spiralling into chaos.

And then there's the hidden, unofficial role that every company secretary inevitably falls into: the corporate compass. People come to you with questions that don't fit neatly into anyone else's job description – because you see the whole organisational structure, and you know how to navigate it. You become the go-to fixer, the one who knows who to call, where to direct things, and how to keep everything moving smoothly behind the scenes.

And, of course, there's the delicate dance with shareholders. No director wants to walk into a board meeting only to find out that a conversation gone wrong has rattled a key investor. Managing those relationships, ensuring transparency while avoiding unnecessary friction, is just another layer of the job.

The role is more than just governance alone. It's balance. It's control. It's knowing that in a room full of power players, the most powerful tool you have is your ability to manage information – both what's shared and what's kept in the vault.

The company secretary: A role without a true home

I think the company secretary function is an anomaly. It doesn't neatly belong in the legal team, nor does it fit within compliance, risk, or the finance department. It's a role that operates in its own sphere, touching every part of the business while never fully belonging to any department.

I sit within the wider group legal team, yet the irony is, I interact more with human resources, investor relations, treasury, and other corporate functions than I do with my legal colleagues. It's not that legal isn't important – it's just that the nature of company secretarial work reaches far beyond it. Governance is its own beast, answering to the board, shareholders, and regulators, not just internal management.

This lack of a natural home is both a challenge and an advantage. Unlike a role that sits firmly in finance or legal, where you're surrounded by like-minded professionals with aligned objectives, the company secretarial function operates across departments, meaning you're constantly navigating different priorities, personalities, and expectations. You don't get caught up in the internal politics of one division, but at the same time, you're interconnected to so many but belonging to none.

Who does the company secretary report to?

Where the company secretary sits within an organisation varies widely. In financial services, they often report to the chair. In other industries, they may report to the CEO or the finance director. I've had a direct reporting line to the CEO, but my strongest reporting relationship has always been with the chair – and that makes sense. A company secretary's real duty is to the board, not just the executive team.

This separation is critical. When a company secretary is too closely tied to management, they risk being pulled into executive-level politics. That's why some company secretaries don't sit on Executive Committee (ExCo) – they might attend meetings but aren't formal members. It's a double-edged sword. Not being on ExCo can mean missing key conversations early on, but being too embedded in the executive team can create conflicts of interest.

Some companies choose not to include the company secretary in the Executive Committee (ExCo) to maintain their independence and avoid potential conflicts of interest.[64]

LEADERSHIP LESSON

The company secretary needs access to the board and freedom from executive influence to do their job well. Reporting directly to the Chair (not the CEO) ensures they can support the board objectively, raise concerns without fear, and protect the integrity of governance processes.

The frustration of knowing too much

One of the biggest unspoken challenges of this role is watching decisions unfold when you already know the outcome.

I've sat in meetings where an executive passionately pitches an initiative, convinced it will sail through board approval. Meanwhile, I know – without a shadow of a doubt – that it's never going to pass. It was rejected last month, last year, multiple times before but their egos get in the way, and they think they're special and have a new way of getting it done. I sit there, nodding along, knowing this conversation is ultimately futile.

There's no point in saying outright, "This is a waste of time." That's not how corporate dynamics work. Instead, you wait. You let the discussion play out. And eventually, reality catches up. Unfortunately, some CEOs sit on a pedestal and don't always have the headspace between their grand ideas to pepper in a reality check and they definitely don't want to hear it from you! It's another one of those water-cooler moments – you know the inside track, but you have to keep a straight face.

A career built on adaptability and learning

If there's one thing I've learned, it's that the role of a company secretary is constantly evolving. Some days, it feels like second nature; other days, I feel like I'm still at the beginning of my journey.

I don't have a singular motto that guides me, but I do know this: learning never stops. Whether from board members, senior executives, or junior colleagues, there's always something to absorb, something to refine.

As the workforce changes and new generations step up, the way we work is shifting. Expectations are different. Priorities are evolving. Adapting to that change is just as important as knowing the rules of governance.

83% of employees worldwide now prioritise work-life balance over pay, marking a significant shift in workplace values.[65]

At the end of the day, the company secretary is more than a title. It's a balancing act — between tradition and innovation, discretion and influence, authority and neutrality. And the best in the field? They're the ones who never stop learning how to walk that line.

LEADERSHIP LESSON

The best governance professionals know that to stay ahead in a role that never stands still, you have to move with it — stay inquisitive, humble, and never stop scanning the horizon for what's coming next.

A constantly shifting landscape

Despite the chaos, the weight of responsibility, and the knowledge that job security can sometimes feel like an illusion, this career has given me an unparalleled vantage point. I've witnessed the best and worst of leadership — CEOs who command a room with vision and authenticity, and those who falter under the weight of their own ego. I've seen boardrooms that thrive on collaboration and others so dysfunctional they crumble.

Through it all, I've learned that true leadership isn't about power — it's about listening, adapting, and making decisions with integrity. And in my own way, whether managing a team, advising a board, or simply ensuring that the right questions get asked, I strive to bring that same ethos into every aspect of my work.

The reality is, no two days in this job are ever the same, and no two challenges can ever be met in exactly the same way. Governance is a constantly shifting landscape, shaped by regulations, economic forces, and the personalities of those in power. But that's what keeps it interesting. Even after years in the field, I'm still learning, still adapting, still figuring out how best to navigate this complex, high-stakes world. And while the journey has been far from easy, with its fair share of absurdity and frustration, I know this much: I'm exactly where I'm meant to be.

LEADERSHIP LESSON

Governance offers a front-row seat to the full spectrum of leadership — the visionary, the flawed, the brave, and the uncertain. It's not a role for those chasing perfection or applause. Stay grounded in purpose, build trust across the organisation, and remain curious.

CHAPTER 8

CHAPTER 8

DANCING WITH GIANTS

I always tell myself the quiet period is coming. Just get through the next two weeks. Just wrap up the board meetings, sign off the annual report, close out the transaction, and then – finally – there'll be a lull. A moment to breathe.

It's a lie, of course. The next thing always comes hurtling towards me, faster than I expect. Another deal, another crisis, another strategic shift that sends the entire organisation into a frenzy. Governance isn't just about rules and regulations – it's about keeping the machine moving, anticipating the next storm before anyone else even realises the clouds are gathering.

I was thinking about that the other day, talking to my parents. They're retired now. Worked their whole lives in a small, tight-knit business – fifteen people, max. The kind of place where decisions were made over lunch, and an argument could be settled by simply looking someone in the eye. They don't really understand the world I work in.

"Why don't you all just agree to stop doing it if it doesn't work?" my dad asked, half-joking but genuinely perplexed.

I laughed, shaking my head. "Because that's not how it works in a corporate."

He doesn't get it – how a single policy, drafted years ago, can become a sacred text, impossible to alter. How decisions get tangled in layers of hierarchy, passing from boardrooms to committees to executives, each adding their own hesitations and revisions. How something as simple as selling a business in Greece becomes an intricate dance of transactions, general meetings, regulatory signoffs, and shareholder politics.

"It's fascinating," I said, knowing full well that 'fascinating' was the wrong word. Maddening, maybe. Exhausting, definitely. But also… intoxicating. Because here's the truth: I thrive in this chaos.

I wasn't raised in a world of polished boardrooms and corporate strategy sessions. My family didn't talk about market caps or shareholder value over dinner. We weren't the kind of people who worried about executive pay structures or strategic divestments. They had stable jobs in a small business, where everyone knew everyone, and success was measured in years of service rather than balance sheets. And yet, here I am.

I've spent the last twenty years navigating some of the biggest corporate machines out there, constantly moving three, six, twelve months ahead, always chasing the next deadline, the next board cycle, the next deal. The corporate world is relentless, unforgiving, and impossible to switch off from. But it's also where I've built my life, carved out a career, and learned to play the game better than most.

Sometimes, when I'm in the thick of it – signing off on yet another round of reports, gearing up for yet another crisis – I wonder what it would have been like to have taken a different path. A simpler one. A quieter one. Then I shake my head, check my inbox, and dive right back in. Because the truth is, I don't think I'd want it any other way.

LEADERSHIP LESSON

Where lawyers look for the right answer, governance professionals know the answer isn't always clear – and that's where they lead. In the grey areas where law, risk, people, and politics meet, it's their judgement, not just their knowledge, that shapes the right path forward.

Accidentally finding my purpose

If you had asked my fifteen-year-old self what I wanted to be when I grew up, the answer definitely wouldn't have been *a company secretary*. In fact, I had no idea such a role even existed. I wasn't one of those kids who had their entire career mapped out, no grand plan for climbing the corporate ladder. If anything, I was just looking for an easy way to make a bit of extra cash. It all started with a ridiculous school rule.

In senior school, we were told we had to do a week of *unpaid* work experience. This was devastating to me. I already had a paper round. I worked in a bar, collecting glasses. I was out there earning, so why on earth would I want to give up a week of paid work to go and work for free? I was *not* impressed.

So, in a fit of teenage rebellion, I decided to game the system. My aunt was a company secretary – not that I had the faintest idea what that meant, but she lived near the beach on the South Coast. That was all I needed to know. I rang her up and said, "Can I come and stay with you? I'll come into your office for a couple of hours a day, then spend the rest of my time on the beach." In my mind, I had outsmarted the system. A free holiday under the guise of career development.

Except... it didn't quite go to plan. When I turned up at her office on the first morning, she looked at me and said, "You're staying here all day, otherwise I'm not signing your form." And that was that.

The unexpected spark

Her job wasn't what I do now. She was the company secretary for a small estate agency on the south coast of England, handling things like building insurance, disability access ramps, and general administration. It wasn't FTSE 100 governance, but it was the beating heart of the business. And despite my best efforts, I found myself fascinated.

People came to her for everything. She knew how things worked. She *ran* things, quietly, efficiently, and without the need for recognition. She was the glue holding it all together.

I fell in love with that idea – the person who sits at the centre of it all, who sees the bigger picture, who makes sure the wheels keep turning. I left that week knowing exactly what I wanted to do.

LEADERSHIP LESSON

A governance professional is the connective tissue of an organisation, interfacing with all departments and stakeholders. Embrace this central role by actively engaging across functions, fostering transparency, and facilitating informed decision-making to drive the organisation forward.

Trying to break in

Of course, knowing what you want to do and actually getting into it are two very different things. By the time I finished university with a law degree (a *broad* choice to keep my options open), I was one of the very few people who actively wanted to be a company secretary. Most of the people I met in the field had fallen into it by accident – former executive assistants, risk analysts, people who just happened to land in a company secretary team and stayed. I wasn't like them. I was determined. And yet… I couldn't get in.

The handful of company secretary recruiters at the time were polite but utterly useless in finding me a trainee role. There were maybe four or five entry-level positions a year, and none of them were coming my way. So, I did what any stubborn, slightly desperate graduate would do. I pulled out the FTSE 100 list from the newspaper, started cold-calling Company Secretarial teams, and offered to work for free. Nothing.

I was *this close* to giving up when I got my break. A recruiter got me an interview at a global bank. I didn't get the job. I came *second*. But something unexpected happened. The hiring manager saw something in me. She liked my determination, my sheer bloody-mindedness in wanting to be in the profession. She went to her boss and said, "This candidate didn't get the job, but I think we need to hire her anyway and take on two new members of the team instead of one." And just like that, I was in.

Looking back, it's wild to think that if my school hadn't forced me into unpaid work experience, if my aunt hadn't put her foot down, if I hadn't been so annoyed about the whole thing – I might never have found this path. Funny how life works, isn't it?

72% of professionals say stepping outside their comfort zone led to career-defining growth, and 49% discovered a new passion or direction as a result.[66]

Becoming indispensable

When I finally got my break at the global bank, I knew I couldn't waste it. It was just a six-month contract, a chance to get my foot in the door – nothing guaranteed. But I wasn't about to let this opportunity slip away. On day one, I made a decision: *if they ever have to consider cutting someone, it won't be me!*

I was the first person at my desk every morning before 8 a.m. I stayed ridiculous hours into the evening, long after others had gone home. If the phone rang, I answered it. If someone needed photocopies, I didn't just do it – I read everything while I stood at the machine, absorbing board papers, committee reports, shareholder notices, anything I could get my hands on.

I became *Little Miss Can I Help?* Literally. One of my colleagues, a rather unpleasant man, started calling me that behind my back. I wasn't supposed to be there, just a contract worker, an afterthought. But I didn't care. *Fine. Let them think I'm overeager. Let them underestimate me.* Because I knew how hard it had been just to get in. And I wasn't going anywhere. And it worked. At the end of the six months, they asked if I wanted to stay. I braced myself for just another extension – but they offered me a permanent job. I was in (again!).

The ultimate training ground

It wasn't just a bank – it was a global financial powerhouse. And despite the sheer scale of the company, our company secretarial team was surprisingly small. Just seven of us handling everything. Which meant I wasn't siloed into one narrow function – I got exposed to everything.

I worked on shareholder governance. I handled board work and committees. I learned the intricacies of international stock-exchange regulations – because the bank wasn't just listed in the UK. We had listings in Asia and the USA, each with different requirements, different regulatory landscapes, different cultures.

I travelled – to Africa, to Asia, working with subsidiary boards, helping roll out governance policies across twenty-five international banking entities. The time zones were brutal – emails from Singapore and Hong Kong flooded in before I was even awake; the Americans were calling just as I was trying to go home – but I thrived in it. And I wasn't just learning about governance – I was learning about people.

I started managing others – first informally, then officially. I was put in charge of a team, responsible for ensuring everything from bank account changes to power of attorney documents ran smoothly. It was trial by fire, but I loved it.

I had incredible mentors, who supported me, encouraged me, and let me take on more responsibility than I probably should have at my level. But that's why it worked – because I grabbed every opportunity, no matter how intimidating. I built processes that lasted long after I left. At one point, after I had moved on, I got a call from my old team – the changes I had implemented were still in place. That meant something to me.

LEADERSHIP LESSON

Engaging in international work exposes governance professionals to diverse cultures, regulatory environments, and business practices. Navigating different time zones and cultural expectations enhances adaptability and broadens one's perspective.

Knowing when to leave

I could have stayed at that bank forever. I loved the work, the travel, the team. But after eight years, I knew I had hit a ceiling. Other people at my level were earning *way* more than me. They held more senior job titles than me, yet I was carrying the same level of responsibility. It wasn't resentment – I just knew if I wanted to keep growing, I had to leave. It was a heart-wrenching decision. I didn't even want to look for another job. The hours were already intense – when was I supposed to interview? And truthfully, I was exhausted.

So, I made a radical decision. I quit. No job lined up. No plan. Just time – time to think, time to breathe, time to figure out what was next. People were shocked. "What's wrong? Why are you leaving?" they asked. And my answer was simple: *Nothing is wrong. Everything is great. But it's time for a scene-change.* For the first time in my life, I wasn't working towards the next deadline, the next role, the next move. For the first time, I just… stopped. And I had no idea what was coming next.

Taking a breath…

After years of relentless work, I did something unthinkable: I took a break. And I didn't do it half-heartedly. In 2011, I had twelve holidays. Skiing in January. A week in the Middle East. Backpacking across Asia – alone. Rugby World Cup in New Zealand. A whirlwind of adventure, movement, and indulgence. I wasn't away for months at a time, but I crammed everything in. There were a lot of pints and there was very little exercise, and I loved every second of it. It was the first time I had ever stepped back and thought, *what do I really want?*

Somewhere in the middle of China, high up in the mountains, my phone rang. A former company secretary was on the line. "Hello," he said. "I understand you're just floating around not doing anything useful. Want to come to Ireland for six weeks?" Turns out, he had someone in his team who needed to step away, and they were in their busiest time of the year. He needed a safe pair of hands. I laughed. "Sure, I'm not doing anything useful." And just like that, I was back in the game.

What was meant to be six weeks turned into five months. This job was completely different from the bank. Another FTSE 100, but a whole different energy. The team was fantastic, the work was engaging, and I genuinely enjoyed it. But it was in Ireland. Ireland is great. But living in Ireland while your life is in London? Not so great.

It wasn't an exciting international move like Hong Kong or New York – it was just enough of a disruption to make life a logistical nightmare. Too many flights, too much time away from home. So when the contract ended, I decided to move on. No full-time job lined up. Just more travelling. I had unfinished business. And New Zealand was calling.

I spent three months in New Zealand, drinking pints, watching rugby, and not working at all. And at some point, between matches and beer-fuelled discussions with strangers, it hit me: I was ready to go back. Not just to work – but to London, to governance, to the career I had stepped away from. I didn't need a radical life change. I didn't want to abandon the profession. I just needed a reset.

Traveling prepares you for the quickly diversifying workforce of today. More than ever, companies are becoming global and diverse.[67]

The luxury fashion gamble

Back in London, it was December, a terrible time to job hunt. The only available role? A temporary job at a luxury fashion brand. Now, let's be clear: I hate shopping. One of my interview questions was, "What do you know about London Fashion Week?" I deadpanned, "Very important week in London." I honestly don't think I would have got the job if they weren't recruiting at a weird time of year. But I went in with zero expectations and, to my surprise, it was fascinating.

The company was a single brand, rare in the governance world. And that meant the way it operated was completely unique. It was creative, fast-moving, and full of talented people.

But it was also too fluid for me. I like structure. I like order. At this company, meetings were chaotic – people would turn up uninvited, decisions would shift mid-conversation, and the governance framework felt more like a suggestion than a rulebook. I stayed for nearly three years – far longer than I expected. But eventually, I missed financial services. I missed the framework, the discipline, the structure. So, I left.

The job that vanished

I thought I had finally found the long-term role I was looking for when I joined an investment company. I was excited. My first permanent role. No more contracts, no more temporary gigs. Six weeks later, they announced they were being acquired. Suddenly, my dream role turned into a non-role. To make matters worse, I wasn't even on the insider list (the record of people within a company who have access to confidential, price-sensitive information that could affect the company's stock price if made public.) This meant I couldn't attend board meetings. So there I was, technically employed, but effectively locked out of doing my actual job. At one point, I found myself packing up archive boxes. That's when I knew it was time to move on.

Investors: Learning a whole new world

Despite the mess at the investment company, I managed to secure a role at an investment management company. This was different from anything I had done before. I had always worked in listed companies – but this was asset management. And I knew nothing about asset management. I didn't know my GPs from my LPs, my LLPs from my investment structures. But that's the beauty of governance – you can move across industries. You can learn new things.

And the investment management company was fascinating. The company had 900 subsidiaries (companies owned or controlled by another company, the parent), mostly set up for property transactions. It was mechanical, complex, full of intricate legal structures – perfect for strengthening my statutory knowledge. I loved it. But then a retailer came knocking.

LEADERSHIP LESSON

Knowing how governance works across borders helps you spot risks, align practices, and strengthen group-wide integrity – it's how good governance scales globally.

Taking the leap into retail

This retailer was a mess when I joined. It had been formed after the merger of two completely different companies that had been shoved together but never truly integrated. One side of the business was losing £70 million a year and dragging the entire company down. I figured it wouldn't stay the same forever – something had to give eventually. Then the pandemic hit. And suddenly, everything changed.

In March 2020, just as the pandemic was sweeping the world, the company made the massive decision to shut down over 500 high-street stores overnight. Advisers warned us, "*This is going to be a Public Relations nightmare.*" *Everyone will say it's the death of the high street.* We braced for impact. I hit the announcement button at 7 a.m. and the London Stock Exchange and all its many investors knew. And then... *nothing.* Nobody cared.

The pandemic was so overwhelming that a FTSE company shutting down over 500 shops barely made the news. It was surreal. Then came April 2020, year-end accounts in a company where every shop was closed, revenue was plummeting, and auditors were questioning going-concern statements. We had to extend our year-end date – unheard of in normal times. Governance became a lifeline, not a back-office function. We worked insane hours, bonded by crisis, navigating the unknown together. And despite the madness, I loved it.

LEADERSHIP LESSON

You can't guide the business through uncertainty if you're not watching the world outside it. Great governance means staying alert to what's changing – and what it means for your board.

Finding my place

This retailer gave me everything I wanted in a governance role. A small, tight-knit team, where communication flows naturally. A place where I could make an impact. Every year, something big happens, and I'm right there at the frontline. And the best part? I got to train and mentor new talent. I've had two trainees at any one time, bringing in young people with little experience and helping them grow into the profession. For me, good governance isn't just about running a board – it's about building the next generation of leaders. And after all these years, I've finally found a role that fits, a profession I love, and a career that still excites me every day.

The unseen strength of company secretarial work

The single most frustrating thing about company secretarial work isn't the long hours, the last-minute board requests, or the relentless cycle of reporting. It's the number of times governance teams are led by people who don't truly understand – or even value – the profession.

I've seen it happen time and time again. You'll have an incredibly strong team, full of experienced professionals who know the business inside out, handling board dynamics, regulatory compliance, shareholder engagement – the real substance of governance. But above them? Someone who doesn't fully grasp what the team does. Someone who may even feel embarrassed by the title of 'Company Secretary', opting instead for something like 'Director of Governance'.

Now, I don't care what people call themselves. If you want to be Chief Governance Architect of the Universe, be my guest. What I do care about is when the person leading a governance team isn't the right ambassador for the profession. That's when the real damage happens.

The CGIUKI Competency Framework sets out the key skills, knowledge, and behaviours governance professionals need to succeed at every stage of their career. It's a practical guide for those who want to deepen their impact and lead with confidence in a complex, evolving landscape.[68]

I've seen brilliant governance teams overshadowed by leaders who don't know enough to speak confidently about governance, who keep the team at arm's length rather than bringing them to the table. They'll take a carefully crafted board paper into a meeting and, when questioned, can't answer a single thing about it – because they didn't write it, and they don't understand it. That's what holds the profession back.

It's not just about how company secretaries are perceived – it's about the barriers we face in changing that perception. If you don't want to do this job, fine. But let those of us who do, get on with it. Let us into the meeting room. Let us present our own work. Let us speak for ourselves.

Because beyond the title, beyond the misconceptions, there's something many still fail to recognise – the depth of technical expertise required for this role. Governance isn't just about guiding discussions and advising on best practices. It's about knowing the law inside out. We are experts in company legislation, and ensuring compliance is a fundamental part of what we do.

The Chartered Governance Qualifying Programme is the only chartered qualification dedicated to governance. It offers in-depth, master's-level training across law, board dynamics, risk, and strategy – setting the standard for expertise in the field.[69]

Not every aspect of our work is high-profile or glamorous, but it is critical. When you've been on the receiving end of regulatory scrutiny, you quickly understand the importance of precise wording, well-documented policies, and meticulous procedural records. These elements ensure that if an issue arises – whether today or years down the line – there's a clear framework in place to address it.

Yet, there's a danger that as governance evolves, technical expertise gets overlooked in favour of soft skills. Of course, both are essential, but statutory obligations, company filings, and regulatory compliance should never be dismissed as secondary. They form the foundation of our profession.

The pace of change in corporate governance is relentless. From ESG developments to reforms at Companies House, staying informed is a constant challenge. No one can claim to know everything, but maintaining technical competence is essential. The best professionals – regardless of seniority – continue to engage with the hands-on elements of their role, ensuring they can guide their teams effectively.

That's why I love seeing new people enter the profession – people who are genuinely excited about governance, who are proud of it, who understand how critical it is. Because the more we champion the value of what we do, the harder it becomes for anyone to ignore it.

Ultimately, we should take pride in every aspect of our work: the advisory role that helps shape corporate governance and the technical expertise that ensures its integrity. One cannot function without the other. And the more we make that clear, the stronger the profession will be.

LEADERSHIP LESSON

Governance professionals blend strategic influence with deep technical expertise – shaping decisions and safeguarding integrity. Those qualified through Chartered Governance Institute UK & Ireland (CGIUKI) commit to a strict Code of Conduct, reinforcing their role as trusted, independent voices at the heart of the organisation.

The role of a company secretary in mergers: One word – Communication

Mergers are another area in which the importance of governance is undeniable – and yet, if you're not paying attention, you could completely miss how much influence the company secretarial team has.

I've walked into organisations post-merger and found next to no integration has actually happened. Two companies legally combined – but operationally? Still running in parallel, completely disconnected. Separate processes, separate policies, even separate printer contracts. And while many people in the business might just carry on as usual, focused on their own siloed roles, a company secretary *has to see the whole picture*.

Governance is the glue that brings everything together. When a merger happens, it's the company secretarial team that ensures decision-making structures align, policies don't contradict, and board oversight, functions as one entity rather than two separate legacies awkwardly bolted together. The secret to making it work? Communication. If you don't communicate – across departments, across leadership teams, across regulatory bodies – then all you have is a merger on paper, not in practice.

A company secretary isn't just someone keeping the legal structures tidy. We're the ones making sure the entire business functions as a single, cohesive entity. And the best ones do it so well that most people don't even realise how much heavy lifting is happening behind the scenes.

The corporate glue: Governance without a manual

When a company undergoes a major transformation, like the closure of a business segment or the shift to an online-only model, people outside the governance world often assume, *that's a commercial decision. What does a company secretary have to do with that?* After all, there's no form to file at Companies House for shutting down part of a business. There's no official governance checklist that says, *this is where the* company secretary *team steps in*. But that's precisely where people misunderstand the role.

A huge part of being a company secretary is owning the group structure – knowing how the entire business is legally and operationally connected. And in any transformation, that knowledge is critical. Because big strategic changes don't happen in a vacuum. They involve layers of complexity – which entities are impacted? Where are employees legally employed? What contractual obligations exist that might complicate things? Who actually needs to be in the room when decisions are being made?

And here's the reality: there's no pre-written process for most of this. Governance professionals often end up owning the work that doesn't naturally sit anywhere else. I've seen this across every company I've worked in – you'll have a mailroom worker show up at the company secretary office saying, "I didn't know where else to bring this, so I thought you'd know what to do with it." And, more often than not, they're right.

LEADERSHIP LESSON
Great governance professionals see the whole system – connecting people, entities, and obligations when others focus only on strategy. Their value lies in stepping into the grey areas, asking the right questions, and quietly holding everything together when the path isn't yet defined.

The company secretary role in business change: More than just paperwork

Did the company secretary team run the business closures? No, of course not. But we played a key role in arming decision-makers with the right information. A huge part of governance is asking the right questions:
- Has someone checked what this means for employee contracts?
- Who legally owns this part of the business, and are there hidden complexities in closing it?
- Which board approvals are required?
- Have we involved the right stakeholders?

It's about ensuring leadership doesn't walk into a decision blind. And in moments of massive business change, that role becomes even more critical. When I started, I took ownership of the corporate structure from day one. Not because it was officially *my* job, but because someone had to. I went out, gathered information, built a repository of knowledge – because that's what governance professionals do. And that's why, even in the biggest transformations, company secretaries are never just bystanders. We're the ones making sure nothing critical gets overlooked.

Employees with high adaptability are 2.5 times more likely to have higher performance and contribute more to the organisation's success.[70]

The power of listening and diplomacy

Company secretaries sit in a uniquely privileged position – we have direct access to senior management, a reporting line that reaches the top, and a seat at the table where major decisions happen. That's not something every role gets, and it's easy to take it for granted. But with that access comes responsibility.

It's easy to complain – to point out what's broken, what's frustrating, what isn't working. But the real value of a company secretary isn't just spotting the problems – it's about finding solutions. It's about presenting issues in a way that leads to action, rather than just another round of boardroom frustration. That's where diplomacy comes in.

You can't thrive in this profession without diplomacy – it's a non-negotiable skill. Every company I've worked in, I've naturally found myself in a position where I help translate frustrations into something constructive. I've volunteered to review employee engagement survey results, to amplify the voices of underrepresented groups, to be a neutral space for those who struggle to be heard – whether it's the parent balancing home and work, the only woman in the room, the junior employee afraid to challenge senior leadership, or just someone who feels like they don't quite belong.

The key isn't just listening – it's figuring out how to package those frustrations in a way that actually leads to change. Instead of saying: *This is annoying, that's broken, and this other thing is unfair*, the questions should always be: *What do I actually want to happen? What change am I asking for? How can I present this in a way that senior leadership will engage with?*

LEADERSHIP LESSON
Governance isn't static – it evolves with every regulation, risk, and boardroom dynamic. A growth mindset keeps governance professionals sharp, open to challenge, and ready to adapt when the rules – or the organisation – change.

Because sometimes the problem isn't the real problem. Sometimes what looks like a broken process is actually a misunderstanding. Sometimes people ask for the wrong things because they don't know what's possible. Sometimes the issue is simply a lack of education – not malice, not resistance, just people not knowing there's a better way. And that's where governance professionals add real value – we don't just keep the machine running, we translate what's really happening into something leaders can act on.

Where do you learn that skill?

Not from a textbook, that's for sure. (*Though if there was a course in "Getting People to Listen Without Them Realising They're Being Managed" I'd sign up.*) Honestly? Life teaches you this. I've had every kind of job – I was a receptionist, a waitress, a bar worker. I genuinely believe everyone should work in retail or hospitality at some point in their life. It teaches you how people behave under stress, how to read a situation, how to de-escalate conflict, how to deal with difficult personalities. It's an education in human nature that you don't get from sitting in an office.

I've told my children – when they're old enough, they need to do it. I don't care if it's a shop, a restaurant, or something else entirely, but they need to experience what it's like to deliver great customer service. It's good for the soul. Because at the end of the day, whether it's a frustrated customer in a café or a tense boardroom discussion, it all comes down to communication. I don't like arguing. It's not my nature. If someone is upset, my instinct isn't to fight – it's to understand. *How did we get here? What's actually going on? What needs to happen next?* That approach has shaped my entire career. And in governance, being able to listen, to translate, and to navigate tensions with diplomacy isn't just useful – it's essential.

LEADERSHIP LESSON

Humility is a quiet superpower in governance. It allows professionals to listen fully, question assumptions, and earn trust – not by being the loudest voice in the room, but by being the most grounded and credible one.

Can you hear me now? and other company secretary joys

Looking back, there have been plenty of laugh-out-loud moments in my career – because honestly, if you don't laugh in this job, you'd cry. One of my absolute favourites was back in my days at the bank, when our company secretarial team was scattered across the world. We were this international, highly professional, highly skilled governance team – and yet, somehow, whenever we tried to have a conference call, it turned into a complete disaster.

This was before Microsoft Teams (which, let's be honest, isn't always perfect either). Instead, we were at the mercy of international telephone lines, which had all the reliability of a dial-up modem in a thunderstorm. So, picture this: Me, in London. Someone else, in Singapore. A few more, dialling in from Africa, Hong Kong, the USA – anywhere with a dodgy connection and a time zone guaranteed to make someone miserable.

And every single call would start the same way:

"Can you hear me now?"
"You're on mute."
"No, YOU'RE on mute."
"Is that an echo?"
"I think we lost David."
"Who's David?"
"Wait, I can only hear every third word – what did you just say?"

It would take a solid twenty minutes just to establish whether we were all actually on the call – let alone discussing the board strategy. And at some point, someone would give up and just start shouting into the void, hoping for the best. But when we finally met in person, all those struggles melted away. Suddenly, these voices on a crackly phone line became real people – people I had spent years working with but had never physically been in the same room with. And that's what I treasure the most – the human side of company secretary work.

The joy (and struggle) of being invisible

The thing about governance is this: when we do our job well, no one notices us. We keep everything running smoothly. We anticipate problems before they happen. We make sure the right people are in the right room at the right time with the right information. And as a reward for doing this flawlessly we become completely invisible. So, when we actually do get recognition, we celebrate it!

One of my proudest moments was an external board evaluation a couple of years ago. The consultant running it – who had done *hundreds* of these evaluations – said something that stopped in my tracks: *"This is the first board evaluation I have ever done where every single board member, without being prompted, specifically praised the company secretarial team for their support."* I nearly fell off my chair. To have every single board member voluntarily bring up how much they value what you do? That's next level. And sure, we could have been modest about it. But nope – I made sure everyone in the team knew. Because let's be honest, this job can be tough.

We get caught in impossible situations. We deal with last-minute crises. We manage high-stakes politics, legal complexities, and leadership personalities *all at once*. And sometimes, we just have to grit our teeth and get through it. But when we get it right? When someone actually acknowledges that we're making a difference? That's the moment to grab a glass of wine (or two) and say: *"See? They noticed. We matter."*

30% of workers have felt invisible at work, and 27% have felt flat-out ignored.[71]

Making the happy moments happen

So yes, there have been naturally happy moments – the friendships, the inside jokes, the moments when something chaotic *finally* comes together. But I also believe in creating those happy moments. We have to support each other – within our teams, within our networks, across the profession. Because if we just sit back and wait for someone else to tell us we're doing a great job, we might be waiting a long time. Instead, we have to celebrate our own wins, back each other up, and keep reminding ourselves why we do this job in the first place. And if all else fails? Just start another board call with: *"Can you hear me now?"* That should get a few laughs.

Governance can feel clinical at times – spreadsheets, policies, board minutes, transactional decisions. But the hardest part of being a company secretary isn't the paperwork. It's the people. My absolute worst moment in this job was one of those situations where no one had done anything wrong – but someone was still going to lose their job. And worse than that? I had to manage the process.

LEADERSHIP LESSON

Sometimes, the real reward is watching others succeed because of something you quietly helped build. When colleagues benefit from a share scheme you shaped behind the scenes, sharing in their joy is a reminder that governance isn't just about managing risk – it's about creating the conditions for people to thrive.

The exit I never wanted to oversee

The person in question wasn't just a colleague. He was a mentor. Someone who had supported me, guided me, given me opportunities when I was just starting out. And yet, for reasons way above my pay grade, a decision had been made, he was leaving. And I was the one who had to project-manage his exit.

I had to map out the entire process – which board roles he was stepping down from, what agreements needed signing, which steps had to be followed if he accepted the terms of his departure... and which ones had to be followed if he didn't. And I had to sit there, in meeting after meeting, listening to people discuss his fate like he was just another administrative task on a checklist. Because that's the thing about governance – when people are reduced to "actions" and "processes," it's easy to forget they're actually human beings. I hated every second of it. I felt powerless. I wasn't senior enough to change the outcome; I couldn't fight for him. The only thing I could do was handle it professionally – make sure the process was as fair and dignified as possible, even when not everyone involved was treating it that way.

Years later, I ran into him at a seminar. My stomach dropped. I had no idea what to say. But before I could fumble out an awkward apology or an excuse to run in the opposite direction, he smiled and said: *"I'm really glad it was you who handled it. I knew you wouldn't have enjoyed it. But you dealt with it well. Thank you."* That just made it worse. I would have preferred if he had been furious. If he had blamed me, been cold, walked away. Anything would have been easier than knowing that he appreciated how I'd handled something I never wanted to handle in the first place.

It's moments like that that make this job brutal. When you have to sit next to people at work, knowing things you can never tell them. When you have to smile and act normal, even when you know layoffs are coming. When you watch decisions unfold that you have no power to stop, but that affect people you respect and care about. And you can't let it show. You compartmentalise. You tell yourself; *It's just business. It's* not personal. But sometimes it is.

LEADERSHIP LESSON

Managing people well isn't optional in governance – it's foundational. The best governance professionals build trust, read dynamics quickly, and adapt their style to bring out the best in others. Mastering this skill means you create the conditions for better decisions and stronger outcomes.

The other tough moments

People assume governance is all about structure and rules, but the hardest part is managing people when things aren't working. I hate it when I have someone on my team who just isn't delivering – when I've tried everything to help, but it's still not clicking. No matter how much you try to support, coach, or guide them, sometimes it just doesn't work.

And that's a horrible feeling. I hate it when difficult decisions must be made – restructures, job cuts, uncomfortable changes. It's never personal. It's never about blame. It's just business. But that doesn't make it easier.

At the end of the day, being a company secretary isn't just about knowing the rules. It's about navigating people, politics, and impossible situations with professionalism and diplomacy. And sometimes, the best thing you can do – the *only* thing you can do – is make sure that when difficult things happen, they happen with dignity. We all deserve that!

Brushing shoulders with the famous (and not realising it)
Beyond the more sombre times, I've worked with high-profile people and have had many moments where I was *supposed* to be impressed. But, more times than I can count, I completely miss the memo and embarrass myself in the process. In some roles celebrity sightings were just part of the scenery. There was even a VIP waiting area, so the rich and famous didn't have to sit with *the little people*. Not that I ever paid much attention – I knew as much about celebrities as I did about fashion, which, as anyone who's ever seen me shop knows, is *not a lot*.

One day my colleague, sent me downstairs to meet someone. I had no idea who they were, but apparently, it was a *big deal*. I turned up, greeted the very well-dressed man politely, and went about my business. Later, back in the office, everyone was laughing at me. "You must have known who he was!" they said. "Nope," I replied. "Should I?"

Turns out, this British actor, with his chiselled jawline and a knack for transforming into historical and eccentric figures, had won an Oscar for portraying a genius. At the time, I genuinely had no clue who he was. Now I do. But back then? He was just another customer in a very nice coat. There were others. A prince came in once, back when he was better known for air miles than anything else. A British supermodel turned actress, known for her bold brows, edgy charm, and effortlessly rebellious style. A British business tycoon, now a billionaire businessman, who revolutionised mobile retail, co-founding a telecom empire that made phones accessible to the masses. And yet, here's the thing – you get used to it.

Board members and executives are treated like celebrities in the corporate world. People whisper about them in the halls, glance over nervously when they pass, act stunned that they actually *know their name*. But at the end of the day, they're just people, and this is every day working in governance.

The human side of the boardroom

If there's one thing that surprised me about working in governance, it's how genuinely kind and supportive many non-executive directors are. Before I started, I had this idea of board members being stiff, intimidating, and impossibly formal – the kind of people who'd correct your grammar mid-sentence and give you a disapproving look if you so much as breathed too loudly. But the reality? They're some of the most down-to-earth, thoughtful people I've ever worked with. Once, I made a silly typo in a board pack – nothing major, but enough to be noticed. One of the NEDs spotted it. Did they call me out in a meeting? Did they cc half the company in an email correction? No. They just sent me a quiet, private message: *Hey, you might want to fix this before it goes out. No worries, just thought I'd flag it for you.* That kind of support makes a difference.

LEADERSHIP LESSON

Taking time to understand what drives people, their "why," transforms conversations from transactional to strategic – and turns resistance into alignment.

Moments that matter

Working for a retailer, I love when we invite members of our customer service team to our AGM (just in case a shareholder turns up with an issue about one of our products). And I love watching board members immediately go over and thank them for their work – without prompting, without an audience, just genuinely appreciating the people on the ground. These directors sit in high-pressure environments, making tough calls, balancing multiple board positions – but the ones I've worked with? They still make time to be polite, to say thank you, to make you feel part of the team. That's what makes all the difference.

On a personal level, I always find it tough when an executive committee member or non-executive director steps down. You build strong professional relationships, sometimes seeing them multiple times a week for years, but once they leave, it's not always appropriate to stay in touch. Unlike with colleagues, you can't just suggest grabbing a drink after work – it's a different world. Still, you care about them and want to know they're doing well. Sometimes, paths cross again on different boards, which is always a nice surprise. Other times, the only reminder of them is a last-minute email in January, asking for help with a tax return.

In Q1 2025, CEO departures from FTSE 100 firms dropped by 67% compared to the same period in 2024.[72]

The other difficult aspect of my career has been the rare but inevitable clash with a manager. I've been incredibly fortunate – of the many bosses I've had, nearly half were guests at my wedding. But there was one individual I just couldn't connect with, no matter how hard I tried. It wasn't just me; others faced similar struggles. Still, I pride myself on being able to improve relationships, even with difficult stakeholders. In this case, despite investing significant effort and emotional energy, I couldn't make any progress.

In a small industry like company secretarial, you always want to be on good terms with those you've worked with. I like knowing I can walk into a seminar and greet everyone without hesitation. But with this one person, I'd feel uneasy crossing paths again. It's frustrating, but ultimately, everything comes down to people – and relationships don't always work out the way you hope.

LEADERSHIP LESSON

Build relationships with care, because trust opens doors – but never forget that people move on. The real value lies in staying professional, adaptable, and anchored in purpose, no matter who's across the table.

The secret ingredient to being a great company secretary

The real secret to excelling in this profession isn't just knowing the law inside out or having an encyclopaedic knowledge of governance codes. It's people. This is a people job, first and foremost. It's about diplomacy, perceptiveness, and knowing when you're about to walk into a minefield. It's about reading a room before anyone even speaks, anticipating problems before they arise, and understanding people well enough to know what they need – even when they don't say it outright. It's about putting out fires before they start.

As of 2025, the Chartered Governance Institute UK & Ireland (CGI-UKI) reports having over 10,000 members across the UK and Ireland at all levels.[73]

A good company secretary isn't just a compliance expert or a governance adviser; they have to be a little bit psychic, too. You need to anticipate what others are going to think and say based on their character and what you know about them. You need to know how it will play out even before they've said a word, then you're prepared and can do your job well. Company secretary's need to balance enthusiasm with realism, positivity with pragmatism. And, crucially, you need to set boundaries.

In a role where relationships matter so much, you learn quickly that trust – while important – has to be earned. That's why my team has a simple, if slightly cynical, mantra: *Trust no one*. Not in a negative way, not because people are deliberately difficult, but because governance is inherently political. Different stakeholders, all with good intentions, can still pull in different directions. And too often, things slip through the cracks.

I've been burned before – by papers that weren't submitted in time, approvals that hadn't really been given, deadlines that were promised and missed. People aren't necessarily trying to mislead; they're just busy, focussed on their own pressures. That's why a healthy level of scepticism is necessary. A smile, a nod, a "Yes, of course, I'll circulate it as soon as I have it" – but never assuming it's done until I've seen it myself.

It's also about accountability. People sometimes think governance professionals should always say yes, should smooth things over, should be facilitators above all else. But sometimes, the most responsible thing you can do is say no.

No, that hasn't been approved yet. No, we can't take that shortcut. No, we won't send that out until it meets the right standard. Saying no isn't obstruction – it's protection. Protection for the board, for the business, for the people trying to get things done properly.

This profession is demanding, unpredictable, and often underappreciated. But for those who thrive in it, it's also fascinating. You're at the heart of how a company runs, privy to the conversations that shape its future. You build relationships at the highest level of business, gain insights that few others see, and develop a skill set that blends legal expertise, strategy, and psychology.

So, what makes a great company secretary? It's not just technical knowledge, though that's essential. It's not just soft skills, though they're invaluable. It's the ability to stand in the middle of it all – balancing diplomacy with decisiveness, trust with verification, enthusiasm with control. It's knowing when to step forward and when to hold your ground.

And for those who get it right, it's one of the most rewarding careers out there.

LEADERSHIP LESSON:
The true strength of a company secretary lies not in knowing everything, but in seeing everything – the people, the politics, the pressure points – and navigating it all with quiet authority. When you blend foresight with integrity, and trust with healthy scepticism, you don't just support good governance – you become its anchor. That's the power of this profession.

Letter to Future Leaders

To those at the helm, those who advise them, and those yet to take the stage. By the time you've reached this final page, you'll have peered behind the boardroom curtain and glimpsed the realities, the contradictions, and the quiet courage that define the world of governance. You've met, albeit anonymously, the men and women who sit at the intersection of power and principle. You've heard their truths – sometimes startling, often humorous, always human.

So now, let's look forward. The role of the company secretary or governance professional is not just a technical function, nor a box to be ticked. It is a calling. A responsibility. A chance to serve as the moral compass, the steady hand, and – when needed – the last line of defence for integrity in leadership.

To CEOs and directors: understand that your governance professional/company secretary is more than a facilitator of meetings or keeper of records. They are your strategic partner. They see what others overlook, feel the mood before it becomes a storm, and absorb complexity to create clarity. A great governance professional is your eyes and ears in moments you didn't know you needed them – and your shield when it matters most.

Invite them in. Listen. Not just when things go wrong, but when everything feels calm. That's often when the seeds of crisis are quietly sown. When the value of the company secretary is overlooked, the organisation loses more than governance support – it loses 360-degree oversight, strategic foresight, and the steady leadership that connects every part of the business.

To Governance Professionals: your work is often invisible, but never unimportant. You are the orchestrator of order, the advocate for transparency, and the quiet challenger of groupthink. Know your value. Speak truth to power with calm courage. Take your place at the table – unapologetically, and with the quiet confidence of one who holds the map while others chase the horizon.

Your presence gives structure to ambition. Your questions refine strategy. Your integrity protects reputations.

To students and newcomers: this is not a job that shouts. It is one that listens, discerns, and speaks only when it counts. It may seem shadowy from the outside, but once inside, you'll find purpose, influence, and a front-row seat to leadership in action. Be curious. Be brave. And remember: the boardroom needs you more than it knows.

This book began with a question — Why doesn't the world know what we do? The answer is not just in these pages. It's in the actions you take after reading them. If one leader pauses to ask better questions, if one student feels seen, if one governance professional stands taller — then this book has done its job.

Let this be more than a diary. Let it be a declaration.

Because good governance doesn't happen by accident. It happens because someone made sure it did.

Be that someone.

With conviction,
Erika Eliasson-Norris
CEO, Beyond Governance

APPENDIX

A brief history of the role of the Company Secretary

The scribe who kept the secrets:
The early Company Secretary

Picture this: it's ancient Mesopotamia, around 3000 BC, and the air smells like dust, sweat, and freshly baked clay tablets. No one's heard of a 'Company Secretary' yet, but the idea's brewing. Back then, if you were a merchant with a stash of goats, grain, or shiny beads, you needed someone to keep track of it all. Enter the *scribe* – the original administrative hero! They scratched numbers and deals onto clay with a reed stylus, making sure nobody stole an extra goat.

Scribes were so well respected that they didn't even get their hands dirty – they had slaves to fan them while they scribbled.[74]

These scribes weren't just number-crunchers either. They were the keepers of secrets, the ones who knew who owed what to whom. If a trader tried to sneak off without paying for his barley, the scribe's tablet was the smoking gun.

Egypt's papyrus

Fast-forward to ancient Egypt, around 2500 BC, where the Nile's flowing and the pharaohs are showing off their pyramids. Scribes here were the rock stars of the reed pen, scribbling on papyrus (fancy paper made from squashed plants). They worked for the temple priests and noblemen who ran massive estates. These estates weren't companies as we know them, but they were *mega-businesses* – think farms, workers, and many assets.

The scribe's job? Record everything: how much grain got harvested, how many workers got paid (usually in bread and beer), and who was slacking off. They even invented shorthand hieroglyphs to keep up.

Egyptian scribes were well educated and knew their value, it's said that they even called everyone else "the unlettered" – basically those who cannot spell! [75]

These individuals were the ancestors of the Company Secretary – trusted, intelligent and the keeper of the truth. They didn't just write things down; they made sure the whole operation didn't collapse into chaos. One wrong hieroglyph, and suddenly the Pharaoh's lost his fortune.

Greece and the gossiping clerks

Now hop over to ancient Greece, around 1200 BC, where the Mycenaeans are busy trading commodities such as olive oil. Their palaces – like the one at Pylos – were buzzing hubs of trade and taxes, and guess who kept it all ticking? The *clerks*! These individuals wrote in Linear B (a language writing system attested to be the earliest form of the Greek language) to track shipments, debts, and who owed the king a sheep.

By 500 BC, the Greeks had moved on. In Athens, they had *grammateus* – secretaries for the city-state's councils. These weren't quite company secretaries, but they set the stage. They took minutes at meetings, managed records, and made sure laws got written down properly.

Some grammateus were former slaves who were so good at their jobs that they were freed.

These Greek clerks were sneaky, too. They knew all the council's dirty laundry – who bribed who, who flirted with whose wife – and kept it locked up tight. Part record-keeper, part secret-hoarder.

Rome's toga-toting tattlers

Ancient Rome, c.500 BC, where the togas are flowing and the empire's growing. Rome's big shots – senators, generals, and rich landowners – had *scribae* to handle their paperwork. These individuals were the ultimate multi-taskers: they wrote letters, tracked taxes, and even doubled as librarians for scrolls full of laws and IOUs.

By 200 BC, Rome had *collegia* – guilds for craftsmen, merchants, and even undertakers. Each collegium had a *scriba* or *secretarius* – Latin for "keeper of secrets." These individuals didn't just count coins; they made sure the guild didn't get cheated and kept meetings on track.

It's been said that some secretarii were so powerful that they bossed their bosses around.

Roman secretarii were the closest we get to a proper Company Secretary before trading companies pop up. They had to be trustworthy (no spilling guild gossip at the tavern), organised (scrolls had to be filed accurately), and tough (they had to have tough conversations with people who didn't like to be told 'no').

The middle ages – Monks, manors, and mayhem

Now we're in medieval Europe, around 500 AD, and the Roman Empire's crumbled. Who picks up the slack? Monks and manor lords! Monasteries were mini-empires, growing crops, brewing ale, and copying books. The monk in charge of records – the *scriptor* – was the unsung hero, tallying barrels of beer and making sure everything was fair.

Meanwhile, feudal lords ran estates bigger than some modern towns. Their *stewards* or *clerks* kept the books – how many pigs got slaughtered, how much rent the peasants owed, and who stole what from whom.

These medieval record-keepers were the last stop before trading companies burst onto the scene. They weren't glamorous – no corner office – but they laid the groundwork. Without them, no one would've known who owned what, and the whole system would've been untenable.

The trading company takeover (1500s–1600s)
Picture this: it's the late 1500s, and Europe's gone trade-crazy. Sailors are swashbuckling across oceans, hauling spices, silk, and gold back home. Enter the *joint-stock companies* – fancy new outfits like the English East India Company (founded 1600), where the wealthy pool their cash to fund risky voyages. And who's keeping this chaotic ship afloat? The Company Secretary, of course! Back then, they weren't called that yet – more like "clerk" or "agent" – but they're doing the job: scribbling charters, tracking shares, and making sure no one steals anyone's assets.

The paperwork pirates (1700s)
By the 1700s, trading companies are everywhere – Dutch East India Company, Hudson's Bay Company, you name it. Secretaries are now proper cogs in the machine, juggling shareholder lists, trade logs, and grumpy investors whining about lost ships. They're the unsung heroes of the *South Sea Bubble* (1720), a stock market flop that ended in catastrophe. The secretaries had to explain why everyone's money vanished. Spoiler: dodgy directors, not their fault!

The industrial age of steam (1800s)
Chug into the 1800s, and the Industrial Revolution's roaring – factories, railways, and steamships galore. Company secretaries are busier than ever, now officially titled as such under laws in the UK *Companies Act 1862*. They're registering businesses, filing annual returns and so much more.

In 1870, a London secretary accidentally mailed a secret merger plan to the wrong company. The result? A rival swooped in, and the deal sank – talk about a paperwork shipwreck! These individuals were so vital that by 1890, the Institute of Chartered Secretaries (now CGIUKI) popped up to train them properly.[76]

The corporate chaos (1900s)
The 20th century's a whirlwind – world wars, stock crashes, and skyscrapers shooting up. Company secretaries are the glue holding sprawling corporations together. They're drafting board meeting minutes, supporting on tax investigations, and wrestling with typewriters that jam mid-sentence. During the 1929 Wall Street Crash, secretaries worked overtime to tally the wreckage – some say they aged 10 years in a week!

In 1940s Britain, wartime rules meant secretaries had to report "enemy shareholders" (Germans owning British stock). One secretary hid Nazi shares in a dummy company called "Herring & Sons" – caught when a fishmonger got a dividend cheque by mistake!

The digital desk jockeys (2000s–2025)

Zoom to today and company secretaries are high-tech wizards. No more quills; it's all laptops, cloud files, and Zoom calls (mute button optional). They're still filing with regulators – think Britain's Companies House or the U.S. SEC – and keeping CEOs out of jail. Laws like *Sarbanes-Oxley* (2002) in the US made them corporate watchdogs, sniffing out fraud faster than a bloodhound.

Conclusion - The immortal scribe

From clay tablets to blockchain, the Company Secretary has morphed from scribe to governance ninja. They've survived pirates, crashes, and paper cuts galore, all while keeping the corporate world spinning. Today, they're just as much the organisation's "secret-keeper" but with a healthy dose of being at the forefront of governance, culture and ensuring their organisation behaves ethically, considers stakeholders and safeguards the reputations of all involved. They must be trustworthy, sharp, and secretly running the show. In short, the unsung legends that have been saving necks and steering the path to fairer, better run organisations since the dawn of trade!

Becoming a Company Secretary in the UK: A pathway to governance leadership

The Company Secretary is one of the most critical roles in UK corporate governance, acting as a bridge between the board, shareholders, and regulators. Far from the outdated perception of a mere administrator, today's Company Secretary is a strategic adviser, a compliance expert, and a guardian of corporate integrity.

For those considering a career in governance, becoming a Company Secretary offers a unique blend of legal, financial, and leadership responsibilities. But how does one enter this profession? What qualifications are required? And what skills make a great Company Secretary? This chapter explores the journey to becoming a Company Secretary in the UK, the qualifications needed, and the realities of the role.

What does a Company Secretary do?

In the UK, company secretaries are responsible for ensuring that an organisation complies with its legal and regulatory requirements, operates transparently, and maintains high governance standards. Their key duties include:

Governance Leadership
- Advise the board on corporate governance best practice, including compliance with the UK Corporate Governance Code (as applicable).
- Support board and committee effectiveness, including meeting planning, performance evaluations, and succession processes.
- Ensure the board operates with integrity, independence, and a long-term strategic focus.

Statutory and Regulatory Compliance
- Oversee statutory filings, maintain company registers, and ensure timely submissions to Companies House and regulators.
- Monitor legal and regulatory developments, ensuring the organisation's policies and reporting remain up to date.
- Support accurate and compliant disclosures, including annual reports, ESG statements, and market announcements.

Board and Meeting Support
- Organise and manage board, committee, and shareholder meetings
- Prepare agendas, coordinate papers, attend meetings, and draft accurate and timely minutes.
- Facilitate informed board discussions by ensuring access to high-quality governance information.

Shareholder and Stakeholder Engagement
- Manage relationships and communications with shareholders, including AGM preparation and share administration.
- Support the board in engaging with wider stakeholders, including regulators, employees, and civil society groups.
- Promote transparency and accountability in line with the organisation's values and purpose.

Risk, Ethics, and Sustainability
- Provide guidance on corporate risk management frameworks and appetite.
- Champion ethical conduct, responsible decision-making, and business integrity.
- Support sustainability strategy and ESG integration into governance processes.

While the role is most commonly associated with large listed companies, company secretaries also work in private companies, charities, public sector organisations, and professional service firms.

The qualifications and pathways to becoming a company secretary

There is no single route into the profession, but the most recognised pathway in the UK is through the Chartered Governance Institute UK & Ireland (CGIUKI), formerly known as the Institute of Chartered Secretaries and Administrators (ICSA).

1. Professional qualifications: The CGIUKI is the leading professional body for governance professionals, offering structured qualifications for those looking to enter or progress within the field. The two primary qualifications are:

The Chartered Governance Qualifying Programme
This is the flagship qualification for those seeking to become a Chartered Governance Professional or Chartered Company Secretary.

The programme covers:
- Corporate Governance
- Company Law
- Risk Management
- Boardroom Dynamics
- Financial Reporting and Strategy

Upon successful completion, individuals gain chartered status, marking them as highly qualified governance professionals.

The Level 4 and Level 5 Certificates
For those starting out or looking for a foundation in governance, CGI-UKI offers certificates in corporate governance, company law, and risk management. These can be stepping stones toward the full chartered qualification.

2. Legal and finance backgrounds
While the chartered route is the most direct, many company secretaries enter the profession from legal, finance, or compliance backgrounds. Solicitors, accountants, and other professionals often transition into the role due to their expertise in corporate regulation.

3. On-the-job training and apprenticeships
Some organisations offer company secretarial apprenticeships or graduate training schemes. These provide practical experience alongside professional study, allowing individuals to work within governance teams while gaining their qualifications.

Skills and traits of a successful company secretary
While qualifications are essential, the best company secretaries possess a unique blend of technical knowledge, interpersonal skills, and strategic thinking. The role requires:
- Attention to Detail: Ensuring regulatory filings, board minutes, and governance reports are precise and error-free.
- Legal and Financial Acumen: Understanding UK company law, the

UK Corporate Governance Code and others, and financial reporting requirements.
- Discretion and Integrity: Handling confidential information and acting as a trusted adviser to the board.
- Communication Skills: Translating complex regulations into clear, actionable advice for directors and executives.
- Adaptability: Navigating an ever-changing governance landscape, from ESG (Environmental, Social, and Governance) requirements to digital transformation.

The realities of the role: What to expect

Becoming a Company Secretary is a rewarding but demanding career. Some key aspects to consider include:
- Fast-Paced Environment: Governance professionals must stay ahead of legal changes, shareholder expectations, and regulatory updates.
- Boardroom Influence: The role provides exposure to senior decision-making, making it a fantastic career for those who enjoy working with leadership teams.
- Continuous Learning: Governance is constantly evolving, so ongoing professional development is essential. Membership with CGIUKI provides access to training, industry updates, and networking opportunities.
- Diverse Career Options: The skills of a Company Secretary are transferable across industries, from FTSE 100 companies to non-profits and government organisations.

Conclusion: A career with purpose and influence

For those with a passion for corporate governance, law, and business strategy, becoming a Company Secretary is a highly rewarding career path. It offers the opportunity to work at the heart of decision-making, influence corporate integrity, and shape the future of organisations.

With the right qualifications – particularly through The Chartered Governance Institute UK & Ireland – and the necessary skills, aspiring governance professionals can build a successful career in this dynamic and ever-evolving field.

For anyone considering the journey, one thing is certain: the role of the Company Secretary is more critical now than ever, ensuring that businesses operate with transparency, accountability, and a commitment to good governance. If you decide to take this path, I wish you all the best, if you choose the right opportunities, you won't be disappointed.

Acknowledgements

This book wasn't written from the centre of my own story, but from the edge of many others. It's a reflection of the experiences shared with me – the quiet moments, sharp lessons, and unexpected truths I've witnessed through the privilege of sitting close to leadership, decision-making, and transformation.

This book is shaped by the people who have shared their voices and truths – fragments of a profession that hides its complexity behind quiet competence. My role has simply been to make sense of what too often goes unseen. Because governance, at its core, is not just a system of rules – it is a study of people: their decisions, their blind spots, their courage, and the quiet influence they wield when no one is watching.

To those who contributed to this book – and to every company secretary who has shared their experience with me throughout my career – thank you. You've reminded me that quiet impact is still impact. Your calm under pressure, resilience in the grey areas, and humour in the face of absurdity have shaped not only how I work, but how I lead. I'm honoured to share your stories, so others may see themselves in your words – and feel seen, strengthened, and less alone.

To every board, chair, CEO, and colleague who challenged me (and occasionally drove me mad): thank you. You gave me my own stories, insights, and scars that enabled me to relate to the contributors in this book. I am grateful for your trust, even when it was hard-earned.

To my team at Beyond Governance – the ones I've led and the ones who've taught me – everyday you remind me that good governance starts with good people, I couldn't do this without you all. Special thanks go to Hayley Goodhew without whom this book would not have been completed.

And finally, to my family: thank you for being endlessly patient, honest, and proud. Thank you to Helena and Emilia, my daughters, for reading my first draft and giving constructive feedback like only 10-year-olds can - directly!

Footnotes

[1] The Chartered Governance Institute UK & Ireland, "The Company Secretary: Building Trust Through Governance," 2020

[2] Health and Safety Executive (HSE), Annual Work-Related Ill Health and Injury Statistics for 2022/23. Published November 22, 2023. Available at: HSE Media Centre

[3] Volkov, Michael, "Boeing's Board Governance Failures and the 737 MAX Safety Scandal (Part III of IV)." Corruption, Crime & Compliance, November 26, 2021. Available at Volkov Law.

[4] Ross, A. (2016) 'Half of women in UK have been sexually harassed at work, study finds'. The Guardian. Available at: https://www.theguardian.com/lifeandstyle/2016/aug/10/half-of-women-uk-have-been-sexually-harassed-at-work-tuc-study-everyday-sexism

[5] ESGWise. (2023) '21 key statistics demonstrating ESG benefits for businesses'. ESGWise. Available at: https://esgwise.org/21-key-statistics-demonstrating-esg-benefits-for-businesses

[6] Department for Business, Energy & Industrial Strategy, Department for Business and Trade, Badenoch, K. and Caulfield, M. (2023) 'FTSE 350 hits boardroom gender balance target three years early'. GOV.UK. Available at: https://www.gov.uk/government/news/ftse-350-hits-boardroom-gender-balance-target-three-years-early

[7] Heuer, R.J. (1999) Psychology of Intelligence Analysis. Washington, DC: Central Intelligence Agency.

[8] Zaghmout, B. (2022). Companies with emotionally intelligent managers make more money. HR News. https://hrnews.co.uk/companies-with-emotionally-intelligent-managers-make-more-money

[9] PwC. (2023). Global Crisis and Resilience Survey 2023. Retrieved from https://www.pwc.com

[10] Applied Corporate Governance. (2020). The UK Stewardship Code: simply redundant bureaucracy? https://www.applied-corporate-governance.com/uk-stewardship-code-redundant-bureaucracy

[11] Association of Certified Fraud Examiners (ACFE). (2022). Report to the Nations: 2022 Global Study on Occupational Fraud and Abuse. Retrieved from https://www.acfe.com/report-to-the-nations/2022

[12] Estimate based on trends observed in the corporate governance sector and insights from professional bodies such as the Chartered Governance Institute UK & Ireland (CGI). The postgraduate qualification is only provided by the CGI.

[13] Resumeble. (2019) 'Company culture: The important role that it plays in employee satisfaction'. Resumeble. Available at: https://www.resumeble.com/career-advice/company-culture-the-important-role-that-it-plays-in-employee-satisfaction

[14] Hubstaff. (2024). Work-Life Balance Statistics for 2024: A Global Perspective. Retrieved from https://hubstaff.com/work-life-balance-statistics-2024.

[15] HR News. (2024, January). 88% of UK workforce have experienced burnout in the past two years. Retrieved from https://hrnews.co.uk/88-percent-uk-workforce-experienced-burnout.

[16] Trades Union Congress (TUC). (2024). British workers putting in longest hours in the EU, TUC analysis finds. Retrieved from https://www.tuc.org.uk/longest-hours-eu

[17] Stonehaven International. (2018) 'Governance and the role of the Company Secretary – March 2018'. Available at: https://www.stonehaveninternational.com/governance-and-the-role-of-the-company-secretary-march-2018

[18] UK Business Mentoring. (2023). Top Six Reasons Why Businesses Fail [Updated 2023]. Retrieved from https://www.ukbusinessmentoring.co.uk

[19] World Economic Forum. (2023). Global Risks Report 2023. Retrieved from https://www.weforum.org/reports/global-risks-report-2023

[20] Cadbury, A. (1992). The Report of the Committee on the Financial Aspects of Corporate Governance. London: Gee and Co. Ltd.

[21] Harvard Business Review. (2016). M&A: The One Thing You Need to Get Right. Retrieved from https://hbr.org

[22] Based on general leadership principles outlined in literature such as Stephen M.R. Covey's The Speed of Trust and various leadership studies from Harvard Business Review.

[23] Flowtrace. (2024). 50 Surprising Meeting Statistics for 2024. Retrieved from https://www.flowtrace.co

[24] KPMG. "Mandatory ESG reporting is here." KPMG UK, 2022. Available at: https://home.kpmg.com

[25] Humor That Works. "Humor at Work Infographic." Humor That Works, 2024. Available at: https://www.humorthatworks.com

[26] Hedley May. Board Agility – Oiling the Machine: The Role of the Company Secretary in FTSE 100 Board Performance. October 2021. Available at: https://hedleymay.com/wp-content/uploads/2021/10/HM_Board-Agility_Oiling-the-machine.pdf

[27] This reflects poor governance, yet it's a request frequently – and inappropriately – made of the company secretary.

[28] Nakamura, Reid. "11 Companies That Created Their Own PR Nightmares (Photos)." The Wrap, April 10, 2017. Available at: https://www.thewrap.com

[29] Experian UK. (2022) Businesses at risk: Survey exposes gaps in UK businesses' crisis readiness plans. Available at: https://www.experian.co.uk/blogs/latest-thinking/fraud-prevention/businesses-at-risk-survey-exposes-gaps-in-uk-businesses-crisis-readiness-plans

[30] Mental Health Foundation, Workplace Stress: 2023 Survey Results, https://www.mentalhealth.org.uk/publications/workplace-stress-survey-2023.

[31] Health and Safety Executive (HSE). (2023) Annual statistics on work-related ill health and workplace injuries 2022/23. Available at: https://www.hse.gov.uk/statistics/overall/hssh22-23.pdf

[32] Office for National Statistics (ONS), Who are the hybrid workers? published 2024. Available at: ONS Website.

[33] S.R. Maheshwari, Indian Administration (New Delhi: Orient BlackSwan, 2001), 25.

[34] 18,927 law graduates in 2021-22 (The Lawyer Portal, 'Law Degree Statistics and Facts' (The Lawyer Portal, 2023) https://www.thelawyerportal.com/careers/deciding-on-law/law-statistics-and-facts/) 8,304 solicitor admissions in 2023 (The Law Society, Annual Statistics Report 2023 (The Law Society, 2024) https://www.lawsociety.org.uk/topics/research/annual-statistics-report-2023) and 671 pupillages advertised (Bar Council, Pupillage Gateway Report 2024 (Bar Council, 2024) https://www.barcouncil.org.uk/resource/pupillage-gateway-report-2024-pdf.html).

[35] House of Commons Library, Unemployment by Ethnic Background: August 2024. Available at: House of Commons Library.

[36] Ernst & Young (EY), Parker Review 2024: Improving the Ethnic Diversity of UK Business Leadership (EY, 2024) https://www.ey.com/en_uk/newsroom/2024/03/parker-review-reveals-good-progress-on-ethnic-diversity

[37] Personnel Today, 'Mid-sized UK firms slow to improve boardroom ethnic diversity' (Personnel Today, 18 March 2024) https://www.personneltoday.com/hr/mid-sized-uk-firms-slow-to-improve-boardroom-ethnic-diversity

[38] Parker Review Committee, Parker Review: Improving the Ethnic Diversity of UK Boards 2023 (London: Department for Business and Trade, 2023), available at www.ey.com/en_uk/newsroom/2024/03/parker-review-reveals-good-progress-on-ethnic-diversity).

[39] Institute for Fiscal Studies (IFS), The first step to tackling the gender pay gap is to understand it. Published on August 23, 2016. Available at: Institute for Fiscal Studies.

[40] Mentorink. (2025) 'Mentoring Statistics 2025: Tomorrow's Blueprint'. Mentorink. Available at: https://www.mentorink.com/blog/mentoring-statistics

[41] Financial Reporting Council.

[42] Chartered Governance Institute (CGI), Stress in Governance: Survey Results 2023.

[43] Robertson, I. T., Baron, H., Gibbons, P., MacIver, R., & Nyfield, G, (2000). Conscientiousness and managerial performance. Journal of Occupational and Organizational Psychology, 73(2), 171-180.

[44] Companies Act 2006, Chapter 46. Available at: https://www.legislation.gov.uk/ukpga/2006/46/contents

[45] Cadbury, A. (1992) Report of the Committee on the Financial Aspects of Corporate Governance (The Cadbury Report). London: Gee Publishing. p.49.

[46] Josa, C. (2022), Imposter Syndrome Research Study. Clare Josa. https://www.clarejosa.com/2022research

[47] Lombardo, M. M., & Eichinger, R. W. (1996). The Career Architect Development Planner (1st ed.). Minneapolis, MN: Lominger Limited, Inc.

[48] Investor's Business Daily (2015) Intuition Isn't Just a Feeling – It's a Decision-Making Superpower. 21 October. Available at: https://www.investors.com/news/management/leaders-and-success/intuition-isnt-just-a-feeling-its-a-decision-making-superpower

[49] World Metrics (2023) Psychological Safety Statistics: Data on Workplace Innovation and Performance. Available at: https://worldmetrics.org/psychological-safety-statistics/?utm_source=chatgpt.com

[50] Knight, R.F. and Pretty, D.J. (1997) The Impact of Catastrophes on Shareholder Value. Oxford Metrica, Templeton College, University of Oxford.

[51] PwC (2019) Global Crisis Survey 2019. PricewaterhouseCoopers International Limited. Available at: https://www.pwc.com/gx/en/news-room/press-releases/2019/global-crisis-survey.html

[52] Stonehaven International (2018). Governance and the Role of the Company Secretary. March 2018. Available at: Stonehaven International

[53] Broadleaf Results (2023). Emotionally Intelligent Leadership and Employee Retention. Retrieved from Broadleaf Results.

[54] Forbes Advisor (2023) Digital communication in the workplace: Statistics and trends, 24 August. Forbes Media LLC. Available at: https://www.forbes.com/advisor/business/digital-communication-workplace

[55] Bright Horizons (2024) Modern Families Index 2024. https://www.hrgrapevine.com/content/article/major-study-reveals-working-mothers-pushed-to-breaking-point-bright-horizons

[56] HM Treasury. (2023). State of the Sector: Annual Review of UK Financial Services 2023. UK Government. https://assets.publishing.service.gov.uk/media/64ad6d32fe36e0000d6fa6a9/State_of_the_sector_annual_review_of_UK_financial_services_2023.pdf

[57] Institute of Chartered Accountants in England and Wales (2024) History of the UK Corporate Governance Code. https://www.icaew.com/technical/corporate-governance/codes-and-reports/uk-corporate-governance-code/history

[58] White & Case LLP (2024) FTSE 350 snapshot: AGM key trends – November 2024 update. https://www.whitecase.com/insight-alert/ftse-350-snapshot-agm-key-trends-november-2024-update

[59] Erez, A. and Gale, J. (2024) Being rude at work could actually get someone killed: study. Journal of Applied Psychology. Reported in New York Post, 27 August. Available at: https://nypost.com/2024/08/27/lifestyle/being-rude-at-work-could-actually-get-someone-killed-study

[60] Inner Mileage (2023) Empathy is the last competitive advantage: Why leadership empathy will define the future beyond 2025. 18 September. https://www.innermileage.com/blog/empathy-is-the-last-competitive-advantage-why-leadership-empathy-will-define-the-future-beyond-2025

[61] Topham, G. (2025) Work-life balance more important than pay, say majority of workers – survey, The Guardian, 21 January. Available at: https://www.theguardian.com/business/2025/jan/21/work-life-balance-pay-workers-covid-pandemic

[62] Miller, L. (2025) The hidden emotional burden of leadership – and how top executives overcome it. Forbes, 24 March. Available at: https://www.forbes.com/councils/forbescoachescouncil/2025/03/24/the-hidden-emotional-burden-of-leadership-and-how-top-executives-overcome-it

[63] Morelli, M. and Wang, M. (2020) Impacts of Organizational Culture on Strategy Implementation in Business Enterprises. International Journal of Managerial Studies and Research, 8(7), pp. 95–99. Available at: https://www.arcjournals.org/pdfs/ijmsr/v8-i7/12.pdf

[64] House of Commons Trade and Industry Committee (2003) The Work of the Committee in 2002. Appendices to the Minutes of Evidence. HC 337-II. Available at: https://publications.parliament.uk/pa/cm200203/cmselect/cmtrdind/439/439ap08.htm

[65] Topham, G. (2025) Work-life balance more important than pay, say majority of workers – survey, The Guardian, 21 January. https://www.theguardian.com/business/2025/jan/21/work-life-balance-pay-workers-covid-pandemic

[66] LinkedIn Learning. (2023). 2023 Workplace Learning Report: Building the Agile Future. https://learning.linkedin.com/resources/workplace-learning-report-2023

[67] Joseph, S. V. (2018, December 5). 6 Ways Traveling Makes You a Better Employee. Forbes. https://www.forbes.com/sites/shelcyvjoseph/2018/12/05/6-ways-traveling-makes-you-a-better-employee

[68] Chartered Governance Institute UK & Ireland (2023) Competency Framework. https://www.cgi.org.uk/qualifications-training/competency-framework

[69] Chartered Governance Institute UK & Ireland (2024) Chartered Governance Qualifying Programme. Available at: https://www.cgi.org.uk/qualifications-training/qualifications/qualifying-programme

[70] AQai (2023) Proof of Adaptability: Stats and White Papers Supporting Outcomes of Adaptability. https://help.aqai.io/hc/en-gb/articles/13249296844701--Proof-of-Adaptability-Stats-and-White-Papers-Supporting-Outcomes-of-Adaptability

[71] Workhuman (2022) The Price of Invisibility: Human Workplace Index. https://www.workhuman.com/blog/human-workplace-index-the-price-of-invisibility

[72] Russell Reynolds Associates (2025) Global CEO Turnover Index – Q1 2025. https://www.russellreynolds.com/en/insights/reports-surveys/global-ceo-turnover-index

[73] Chartered Governance Institute UK & Ireland (2025) About us. Available at: https://www.cgi.org.uk/about-us

[74] Bard, K.A. (1999) Encyclopedia of the Archaeology of Ancient Egypt. London: Routledge

[75] Lichtheim, M. (1973) Ancient Egyptian Literature, Volume I: The Old and Middle Kingdoms. Berkeley: University of California Press.

[76] Chartered Governance Institute. (2021) Our History. Available at: https://www.cgiglobal.org/about-us/our-history